SCOTTISH
HIGHLAND HOSPITALITY

With best wishes from
Claire Macdonald

First published 2002
by Black & White Publishing Ltd,
99 Giles Street, Edinburgh EH6 6BZ

ISBN 1 902927 40 0

Introduction and establishment profiles © Claire Macdonald 2002
Recipes © The contributing establishments 2002
All photographs © Stephen Kearney 2002

British Library Cataloguing in Publication data: a catalogue record for
this book is available from The British Library.

With grateful thanks to VisitScotland for their kind contribution towards
the publication of this volume. For more information about Scotland
visit www.visitscotland.com

VisitScotland

Project management by Patricia Marshall
Book design by Creative Link
Layout design by Janene Reid

Printed and bound in Spain by Bookprint, S.L., Barcelona

New Recipes from the
Scottish Highlands and Islands

Scottish
HighlandHospitality

Edited by
CLAIRE MACDONALD
Photographs by
Stephen Kearney

BLACK & WHITE PUBLISHING

We have reproduced the recipes as supplied by the chefs, according to their own individual cooking styles. All recipes serve four, unless otherwise stated.

Contents

Introduction

BY CLAIRE MACDONALD

The Highlands and Islands of Scotland are renowned worldwide for their hospitality. But how does one define hospitality, particularly in such a dramatic setting as the Highlands of Scotland?

Obviously, as with taste, people's perceptions of hospitality vary greatly. A warmth of welcome would undeniably come top of most people's image. But there are numerous other aspects to hospitality which contribute to the depth of welcome. For instance, warmth of temperature is an essential ingredient. When this warmth comes from flaming log fires it is particularly appreciated, as comments from our guests here at Kinloch demonstrate to us time and time again. No matter how friendly staff and owners are to their guests, if the temperature of the building is cold, the atmosphere too will be dominated by the chill.

In parts of mainland Europe, people see flowers as a demonstration of welcome and there can be no doubt that they contribute greatly to the overall atmosphere in a house or restaurant. My abiding memory of Clifton House in Nairn is of the sheer abundance of flowers, with vases in every room throughout the house – drawing rooms, dining room, bedrooms and even bathrooms – all picked from the Clifton gardens. But then, too, there is the food.

When I was invited to edit this book, I thought long and hard about the criteria for the places that I would include. Not everyone will agree with my choice, but after thirty years of running our home as a hotel here in Skye, and very much aware that Godfrey and I are still learning the trade which is our way of life, I feel able to recognise what most people expect in terms of hospitality from any establishment. Which is what we set out to do all those years ago – to make people feel both welcome and at home when staying here at Kinloch; to give them really good food, all homemade; to use our own, organically grown or raised produce wherever possible; and to reflect the seasons. But we do not claim to be chefs. We are cooks in the kitchen at Kinloch, and I strongly believe there is a difference.

So I have followed my own instincts. I have not included any establishment that has had a change of chef in less than a year. I also wanted to write about owner-occupied places, whether restaurant or hotel. The contents of this book reflect my choice. And yet there is a great diversity of place here, from the small and intimate, such as Café One in Inverness, to the altogether more imposing and formal Ackergill Tower. But even in a place that commands a more formal atmosphere, there is a complete lack of obsequiousness and a great depth of warmth and hospitality. Nowhere, however formal in aspiration, can afford to forego a genuine desire to make people feel at home in their establishment.

I find a great weakness for 'guide addiction' within our industry. It is many years ago now that Godfrey and I asked both the *Good Food* and *Good Hotel Guides* not to include us in their books. But as soon as I was asked to do this volume I bought all the guides I could find, to read up and compare the various places I had in mind to include. The variety of write-ups proved to me just how inconsistent guides can be, how they depend on individual attitudes and, to a certain extent, on public relations experts and their influence. The only guide book in Scotland which does justice to the wide number of places it includes is *Scotland the Best* by Peter Irvine.

A further drawback to guiding visitors to Scotland is the grading system of some books, which tend to standardise, thereby neutralising individuality – the very key of Highland hospitality. A couple of places I visited whilst researching this book, anticipating their inclusion from what I had read in other guides, turned out to be lacking in both welcome (in one notable place, the owners seemed monosyllabic) and the quality of their food. It fascinates me that such places can be praised in print, yet offer something quite different in practice.

To write about only twenty places has been very difficult and has resulted in the pruning of many excellent establishments I so badly wanted to include. But I have been allowed a section explaining the somewhat notable absence of places which one might expect to find in a book entitled *Scottish Highland Hospitality* – such as The Three Chimneys here in Skye, The Albannach in Sutherland, and Boath House near Nairn (*see* p. 244). All these exceptional places were included in a recent publication, *Scotland on a Plate*, also published by Black & White. There are also numerous excellent, small eating establishments dotted throughout the Highlands and Islands. So often people tend to confuse quality with cost. True quality is in a bowl of homemade soup and the home-baked bread served with it. This gives far more of a reflection of the local welcome than a main course that sounds enticing on a menu and yet, on appearance, yields a small

stacked heap in the centre of a large plate, with a sauce in neat dots around the edge – an art form in itself, but never enough to truly taste. This sort of food presentation I deplore, and what I find disparaging is that it is perceived as being 'the best' by some people, yet it can rarely reflect the locale, if it is produced in a rural area. Such food I expect to find in city restaurants. But examples of where chefs produce food that is both lovely in presentation as well as reflecting produce local to their area are served in all of the establishments I have written about in this book. For instance, the enchanting, white-washed Kylesku Hotel, situated right above the slipway where the ferry used to cross the waters of Kylesku, serves fish and shellfish, both of which are landed less than ten metres from the hotel door. It is perfectly cooked and served with delicious, complementary sauces and vegetables by chefs untainted by 'city restaurant-itis'. The Summer Isles Hotel similarly epitomises all that I love in its attitude to both food and hospitality, resulting in a paradise of comfort and delicious food. At The Loft, the exceptional restaurant in Blair Atholl, Daniel Richardson makes the most of the abundant local produce. The fact that he can and does go out to pick wild fungi of several types thrills him. He eagerly anticipates the soft fruits season so near to the restaurant, and bemoans the news that a local asparagus grower has this year pre-sold his entire crop to a supermarket chain.

This enthusiasm is all good news to those of us who love our food to the extent that I do. But Daniel is no exception to the other cooks and chefs whose establishments feature in *Scottish Highland Hospitality*. All the owners, cooks and chefs seek out the very best produce they can buy and give due praise and appreciation to their suppliers, an aspect of cooking that is so important and, I feel, not practised enough. I think such appreciation of suppliers perhaps matters most to those of us who work in the Highlands and Islands because, until relatively recently, actually procuring the best foods has not been easy.

I have visited each place in this book, and some I know very well. I was determined before I began that the Islands shouldn't be left out just because it takes that little extra time to get there, and I am so glad I visited Orkney to see The Creel. Lewis and Harris are as different in their landscape as Skye, and the beaches on those islands, especially Harris, are surely some of the most beautiful in the world. The wildlife pretty much everywhere in the remoter places featured in the book – Lewis, Harris, Skye and Kylesku, to name just a few – is a reason in itself to visit. I am blown over again and again by the Highlands and Islands (and all of Scotland, for that matter) and the widely varying beauty on offer

– by the sea, beaches, lochs, rivers, trees, shrubs and wild flowers; by the open, rugged landscapes such as those in Sutherland, Lewis and Caithness; by the glimpse of an otter or a golden eagle. And the food . . . it is just so easy to eat so very, very well. And I think that for me, the food is the most important lure to anywhere. Perhaps it seems that this statement strips away the importance of the welcome, but remember that food in itself is a welcome – it can't be good food if it is mean, created and cooked in a bad atmosphere.

Food is and should be luscious, however simply produced. Its very quality makes it luscious. And some of the best food in the world is produced, caught, grown and cultivated in the Highlands and Islands – which are, after all, the last great wilderness area of Europe. So I hope that you enjoy reading this book and visiting the places in it. I have loved researching each establishment, and seeing and experiencing for myself just how superb is Scottish Highland hospitality.

At Skail House, Orkney

2 Quail

Dornoch

MICHAEL AND KERENSA CARR

Dornoch is a small attractive seaside town in Sutherland. It is famous for its world-ranking golf course, which is only a five-minute walk from 2 Quail, and as well as the fine coastal walks along the beautiful sandy beaches, there are lovely woodland walks nearby.

Michael and Kerensa Carr have owned 2 Quail for five years and, at the time of writing, Michael is short-listed for the Scottish Restaurant Chef of the Year. Situated on Castle Street in the centre of the town, the restaurant comprises two dining rooms on the ground floor of a traditional town house. These warm and attractive rooms are decorated in red and apricot colours and they are filled with books and pictures. There are comfortable and well-appointed letting bedrooms on the first floor above the restaurant as well, not to mention a cosy and book-filled lounge where guests can relax.

The menu at 2 Quail is so tantalising it makes choice extremely difficult. The food is utterly delicious. The excellence of the food lies in the very high quality of the produce, a factor that is common to every establishment in this book. Michael buys his fish from The Fish Platter in Inverness and shellfish from Isle of Skye Seafood, Broadford. His meat comes from J. M. Munro, the butcher in Dingwall, and his fruit and vegetables come from Munro Fruit Merchants in Tain. The cheeses are from J. R. Foods and deli-foods come from Vin Sullivan of Abergavenny. Kerensa buys wines from many sources, including Corney & Barrow, O. W. Loeb, Wine Importers of Edinburgh, and Inverarity Vaults.

The overall impression of both 2 Quail and its rooms is one of warmth and welcome – indeed, of true hospitality.

2 QUAIL

Starter

Scallop risotto
with broad beans and crispy bacon

Wine suggestion: Cuvée des Seigneurs de Ribeau
Pierre, 1998, Gewürztraminer – Trimbach, Alsace
(France) – or other good producers: Hugel,
Kuentz-Baz and Rolly-Gassman

Main course

Roast loin of roe deer
with a brandied cherries, walnut
and thyme sauce

Wine suggestion: Château La Lagune, 1989, Haut-
Médoc (France) – or alternatively Cantemerle or
the other fine bourgeois properties like Cissac,
Lanessan or Liversan with some bottle age

Dessert

Vanilla bavarois
with a raspberry coulis

Wine suggestion: Clos d'Yvigne, 1995, Patricia
Atkinson, Saussignac (France) – or explore other
sweet whites from Cadillac, Loupiac or Barsac

Menu

Scallop risotto

with broad beans and crispy bacon

When buying your scallops, be sure to ask for 'dry' scallops. If your fishmonger tries to sell you 'soaked' scallops, change your fishmonger!

for the scallops
12 scallops

for the risotto
1 shallot, peeled and finely chopped
a little olive oil
300g risotto rice (Arborio or Carnaroli)
salt and freshly ground white pepper
570ml fish stock, enhanced with the
 scallop trimmings
55ml white wine

50ml double cream
25g butter
2 tsp fresh chives, finely snipped
1 tbsp Parmesan cheese, freshly grated

for the garnish
6 rashers of streaky bacon, cut into
 short thin strips
a little vegetable oil
50g broad beans, blanched and skinned

For the scallops: Prepare the scallops by ensuring that the foot muscle attaching each scallop to its shell is removed. Keep four of the best roes whole for garnishing and cut the rest into 1cm dice. Add any trimmings to the fish stock.

For the risotto: In a thick-bottomed pan, sweat the shallot in the olive oil for a few minutes. Add the rice and seasoning and stir well. Bring the fish stock to the boil and gradually add three-quarters of it, allowing the rice to absorb a ladleful at a time and stirring regularly to prevent it from sticking. Continue cooking until the rice is *al dente* (still having a slight firmness) and most of the stock has evaporated or been absorbed. Add the wine, cream, butter, chives, Parmesan cheese and diced scallops to the risotto, taste it and adjust the seasoning if necessary.

For the garnish: Shallow-fry the bacon strips in the vegetable oil until crispy and drain well. Cook the reserved scallop roes in the remaining fish stock for 1 minute.

To serve, place the risotto in bowls and garnish with the hot bacon strips, cooked scallop roes and blanched broad beans.

Roast loin of roe deer

with a brandied cherries, walnut and thyme sauce,
potato rösti and roasted shallots

for the venison stock
venison bones (see below)
1 medium onion
2 carrots
1 stick of celery
2 leeks
1 litre water
250ml red wine
a few juniper berries

for the roast loin of roe deer
800g loin of roe deer (your butcher can
    bone it and give you the bones for
    the stock)
a little walnut oil

for the sauce
570ml venison stock
200g griottines (brandied cherries,
    available in jars)

2 tsp fresh thyme leaves, picked
50g shelled walnuts
25g butter
salt and freshly ground black pepper

for the shallots
12 shallots, peeled
a little vegetable oil

for the potato rösti
2 large Maris Piper or Desirée potatoes
75g clarified butter
salt

for the accompaniments
4 sprigs of fresh thyme
vegetables of your choice

For the venison stock: Brown the bones in a large pot together with the roughly
chopped vegetables. Add the water, wine and juniper berries, bring to the boil and
simmer for 5 hours, skimming off any impurities and topping up the water as
necessary. Strain the stock and allow it to reduce by half.

For the roast loin of roe deer: Preheat the oven to 230°C (gas mark 8). Remove
any fat or sinew from the loin and cut it into four equal portions. Heat the walnut
oil in an ovenproof pan and seal the loin pieces on all sides. Place the pan in the
oven and cook for approximately 12 minutes. Remove the venison loins from the
oven and allow them to rest for 5 minutes.

For the brandied cherries, walnut and thyme sauce: Put the roasting pan back
on the stove, add the stock and reduce the volume by half. Add the drained

griottines, along with two tablespoons of the liquor from the jar, the picked thyme and the walnuts. Simmer until the sauce starts to thicken and then add the butter to give the sauce a glaze. Season it to taste.

For the potato rösti: Peel, wash and grate the potatoes, then pat them dry in a clean cloth. Mix in the salt and half of the butter, then heat up a medium-sized frying pan and add the potato mixture, one layer at a time, adding a little of the remaining butter between each slice. When the underside is brown, turn the rösti over and brown the other side.

For the shallots: Roast the shallots in a hot oven for about 10 minutes.

To serve, slice the venison obliquely and place in a fan arrangement on the 4 serving plates. Surround the meat with the sauce and garnish with the roasted shallots and thyme sprigs. Cut the potato rösti into portions and serve along with vegetables of your choice.

Vanilla bavarois
with a raspberry coulis

for the bavarois

2 egg yolks

75g caster sugar

1 pinch of salt

275ml milk

1 Bourbon vanilla pod, split with the
  seeds scraped out and retained

2 leaves of gelatin, soaked

150ml double cream, lightly whipped

for the raspberry coulis

300g fresh raspberries

110g caster sugar

for the garnish

a few extra raspberries

For the bavarois: Beat the egg yolks, sugar and salt until pale, light and creamy. Put the milk, vanilla pod and scraped out seeds into a pan and bring the milk to the boil. Pour the boiling milk on to the egg mixture and stir everything together. Strain this custard into a clean pan and cook on the stove until it is of a consistency to coat the back of a spoon, taking great care not to let it boil.

Squeeze the water out of the soaked gelatine. Pour the custard into a clean bowl, add the gelatine and mix them together. Allow the mixture to cool in the fridge, whisking regularly until the mixture starts to reach the point of setting. Now gently fold in the whipped cream, pour the bavarois into 4 ramekins and then refrigerate the mixture until it is set.

For the raspberry coulis: Put the raspberries into a bowl and cover them with the sugar. Leave them to steep for about half an hour to allow the sugar to draw out the juices. Put the mixture in a blender, purée it and then pass it through a fine sieve to remove all the seeds. Chill the coulis before use.

To serve, turn the bavarois out of the ramekins on to the 4 serving plates, surround them with the raspberry coulis and garnish with a few fresh raspberries.

Loch Melfort, Argyll

Ackergill Tower

Caithness

ARLETTE AND JOHN BANISTER

John and Arlette Banister have lived at Ackergill for fifteen years and they have totally restored the Tower to its former glory. This fascinating house is in an exceptionally beautiful location close to the Pentland Firth, north of Wick. Positioned directly above a wide bay, whose beaches sweep far out to both the left and right, the views from it are truly spectacular.

Ackergill is not a hotel but a retreat where business people can hold corporate meetings and entertain clients – although it can also be used for private house parties. The genuine Scottish and Highland hospitality that Ackergill offers is perfectly judged – exactly the right balance between conviviality and the formality that is necessary for this type of stay.

The chef at Ackergill is Kevin Dalgleish. He has been there for five years – three as sous chef, then two as head chef. His delicious food is created from the very best seasonal produce – local beef and lamb, fish from the Scrabster fish market and shellfish from Ackergill's own creels in the bay, while many of the vegetables and all of the herbs are home grown. Once a year, a chef visits for several days of demonstrations. In February 2002 the visiting chef was Anton Mosimann, and Paul Rankin has been invited to come to Ackergill in 2003. Inevitably, these chefs go back to their own establishments feeling very envious of the excellent local produce that Ackergill has on its doorstep, although their visits also serve to recharge the culinary batteries of all who attend.

The food is of vital importance at Ackergill but, for the lucky guests, so too is the variety of places where it can be eaten – in addition to serving meals in the splendid dining room, picnics are held on the beach and barbecues can be enjoyed in the fishing bothy. But for all this, Ackergill can surely boast one of the most magnificent dining rooms in Scotland. In this vast oak-panelled room, with fireplaces at both ends and family portraits hanging from the walls, the sense of occasion that this impressive room creates is just dazzling, with guests sitting at a long white-clothed table having been piped to their places. Above all, though, it is the atmosphere at Ackergill that guarantees its success.

ACKERGILL TOWER

Starter

Ackergill shellfish cocktail

Wine suggestion: Sauvignon Blanc, 2001, Thelema
Mountain Vineyard (South Africa)

Main course

Roast saddle of Highland lamb
with tomato fondue, braised cabbage,
fondant potato and a port wine jus

Wine suggestion: Red Bordeaux, 1997, Château
Batailley 5ème Cru Pauillac (France)

Dessert

Iced Halkirk raspberry soufflé
with strawberry, black pepper
and mango coulis

Wine suggestion: White Bordeaux, 1983, Château
Coutet à Barsac, Barsac (France)

Menu

Ackergill shellfish cocktail

At Ackergill we are lucky enough to have our own creel boat. Crab and, on a good day, lobster will be delivered straight to my kitchen door. This recipe allows each individual flavour to be easily identified and enjoyed.

for the mayonnaise	for the shellfish	for the accompaniments
2 tbsp mayonnaise (readymade is fine)	2 x 700g lobster tails	1 ripe mango, peeled, sliced and then cut
a pinch of smoked paprika	2 large scallops	into 12 circles using a
juice of 1 lime	4 langoustine tails	small cutter
	50g white crabmeat	150g baby spinach
	salt and freshly ground black pepper	leaves, stalks removed
for the lemon dressing		salt and freshly ground
juice of 4 lemons	1 tsp caviar (lump fish roe is fine)	black pepper
25g caster sugar		a little aged balsamic
a little arrowroot		vinegar, to drizzle
55ml olive oil		

For the mayonnaise: Blend all the ingredients together.

For the dressing: Put the lemon juice and sugar in a pan, bring them to the boil and thicken by adding the arrowroot. Then whisk in the olive oil and leave to cool.

For the shellfish: Boil the lobster tails in salted water for 7 minutes and, when cool, peel off the shells. Remove the scallops from their shells and steam them, along with the langoustine tails, for 3 minutes. Allow the langoustine tails to cool and then peel the shells off. Place the crab in cold water, bring it to the boil and cook it for 2 minutes. Now plunge the crab into cold iced water to cool it quickly.

Once you have cooked all the shellfish, season it and arrange the scallops, langoustine tails and then the crab meat into a nice tower, topped with the caviar. Divide each lobster tail in two and slice each piece in three places, taking care not to cut all the way through. Slide a mango disc into each cut and place the lobster pieces next to the towers.

To serve, lightly dress and season the spinach leaves, place some opposite the shellfish towers and drizzle the balsamic vinegar and mayonnaise around the plates.

Roast saddle of Highland lamb

with tomato fondue, braised cabbage, fondant potato and a port wine jus

Living, as we do, in the Highlands with green fields full of sheep, I always try to include a saddle of lamb in the menu planning during our guests' visits.

for the fondant potato
4 potatoes, peeled and
   cut into 3cm-thick
   rounds, using a 5cm
   cutter
275ml chicken stock
1/2 bulb of garlic, kept
   whole
110g unsalted butter
1 sprig of fresh thyme
1 sprig of fresh rosemary

for the tomato fondue
4 tbsp herb oil
   (readymade)
2 shallots, peeled and
   finely chopped
1/2 clove of garlic,
   crushed
10 plum tomatoes,
   skinned and deseeded

for the port wine jus
2 shallots, peeled and
   chopped
1 tsp olive oil
150ml red wine
150ml port
1 sprig of fresh thyme
275ml reduced lamb
   stock (readymade)
2 tbsp port wine jelly
   (readymade)
salt and freshly ground
   black pepper

for the pancetta and
   asparagus
40g pancetta, cut into
   small squares
8 spears of asparagus,
   trimmed and peeled

for the lamb
1 short saddle of lamb,
   boned, trimmed of fat
   and cut into 2 loins
salt and freshly ground
   black pepper
1 tsp olive oil, for
   sealing
50g Parmesan cheese

for the braised cabbage
1 cup of ice-cubes
110g unsalted butter
1 savoy cabbage,
   shredded
40g frozen garden peas
6 sprigs of fresh thyme,
   picked to remove
   stalks
salt and freshly ground
   black pepper

For the fondant potatoes: Cook the potatoes first as they take the longest. Put the discs in a thick-bottomed frying pan. Pour in the stock and add the garlic, butter and herbs. Place on a high heat until the stock has reduced and the potatoes start to colour. Expect this to take around half an hour. Once they are cooked, turn them over and keep them warm.

For the tomato fondue: Pour the herb oil into a pan and add the shallots and garlic. Cook for 2–3 minutes without allowing them to colour. Add the tomatoes and reduce to a moist paste. Set the fondue aside until the lamb is cooked.

For the port wine jus: Sweat off the shallots in the olive oil and then add the red wine, port and thyme. Reduce by two-thirds, add the reduced lamb stock and reduce by about half. Now add the port wine jelly, season the jus and pass it through a muslin cloth. Set the jus to one side.

For the pancetta and asparagus: Sauté the pancetta until it is golden brown and crispy and then set it to one side. Blanch the asparagus in boiling salted water for 2 minutes, plunge it into ice-cold water and then set it to one side.

For the lamb: Preheat the oven to 180°C (gas mark 4). Season the lamb loins and seal the meat by frying each surface in hot oil for a few minutes, until they are coloured. Place the loins in an oven tray and roast them in the oven for about 7 minutes. Remove the loins from the oven. Spread the tomato fondant over them, sprinkle the cheese on top and leave them to rest.

For the braised cabbage: While the lamb is cooking, heat a thick-bottomed pan and throw in the ice-cubes and butter, followed quickly by the cabbage, peas and thyme. Stir for 2–3 minutes before adding the sautéed pancetta and blanched asparagus spears. Cook until the butter has glazed the mixture. Season the mixture and immediately divide it between 4 warmed serving plates.

To serve, place the fondant potato at 12 o'clock on the plate, arranging the vegetable and pancetta mixture below them. Slice the lamb, which should be pink, and place the slices on top of the vegetable and pancetta mixture. Drizzle the port wine jus around the plate and serve at once.

Iced Halkirk raspberry soufflé

with strawberry, black pepper and mango coulis

This recipe is a must during the local strawberry and raspberry season. To finish a lovely meal with the freshest taste of good pure fruit and the sweet balance of the soufflé is a joy to the heart as well as the mind. Start this dish the day before serving it as you need to allow at least 12 hours for the soufflé to freeze.

for the soufflé
2 medium egg yolks
75g caster sugar
425ml double cream
25g oatmeal, toasted
  under the grill
300g Halkirk raspberries
  (fresh locally grown
  ones are fine)

for the stock syrup
200g caster sugar
275ml water
juice of 1 lemon

for the strawberry and
  black pepper coulis
250g ripe strawberries,
  hulled and cut into
  pieces
60ml stock syrup

freshly ground black
  pepper, to taste

for the mango coulis
1 ripe mango, peeled and
  cut into pieces
60ml stock syrup

for the garnish
4 sprigs of mint

For the soufflé: Whisk the egg yolks and sugar until the mixture reaches a thick consistency and then put it to one side. Whisk the cream until it forms soft peaks and fold it into the egg and sugar mixture. Add the toasted oatmeal and raspberries, reserving a few for the garnish, and gently mix. Spoon the soufflé into moulds and freeze for 12 hours.

For the stock syrup: Place all the ingredients in a pan and boil them vigorously for 5 minutes.

For the strawberry and black pepper coulis: Blend the strawberry pieces and the stock syrup together and rub the mixture through a sieve. Add black pepper to taste.

For the mango coulis: Blend the mango pieces and the stock syrup together and rub the mixture rub though a sieve.

  To serve, place a soufflé on each of the 4 serving plates, surround them with the reserved raspberries and top with a sprig of mint. Drizzle the strawberry and black pepper coulis and the mango coulis around the plates and present at once.

Croft, Vatersay

The House of Bruar

Blair Atholl

JIMMY McMENEMIE

I used to dream of being able to travel south from Skye without needing to take a picnic. Before The House of Bruar opened there was nowhere on the journey serving good, reasonably priced, food.

As you enter the main building here, you first come to the food hall where only the very best food is sold. It is an Aladdin's cave of potential for present buying and for gluttons like myself, the produce coming mainly from Scotland but such delicacies as shrimps from Morecombe Bay and sticky toffee pudding from Cumbria also being available. You then go through to the elegant self-service restaurant where there is a wide range of delicious cold and hot food on offer. What is so wholly commendable is that, no matter how busy the restaurant is (and in summer months, two to three thousand people come through it during the course of each day), the food remains at a consistently high standard.

The chef in charge of every aspect is Jimmy McMenemie. He has been responsible for the catering at Bruar for the seven years that the restaurant has been open. His brief from Mark Birkbeck, the owner, was to provide British food at its best. And Jimmy does just that. The dressed crab with prawns is a treat to eat and the fish and chips are as good as any I have eaten. The baked ham, carved to order, is excellent and the salads are both interesting and delicious. The range of hot dishes includes roasts, casseroles and pies, and the hot vegetables are so very good that they can form an excellent meal in themselves. Plans are afoot to improve their already delicious sandwiches by doing made-to-order varieties from a special bar. They also aim to increase the fish served and to have a serviced restaurant that will be open for dinners.

Travelling, for whatever reason, is made so very much more acceptable and comfortable when you can look forward to a first-rate lunch along the way!

THE HOUSE OF BRUAR

Starter

West Coast seafood platter
with a dill vinaigrette

Wine suggestion: Sancerre les Rochettes FB,
1999 (France)

Main course

Chicken and broccoli cheese bake

Wine suggestion: Castle Creek Chardonnay,
2000 (Australia)

Dessert

Cooked vanilla cheesecake
with a fruit coulis

Wine suggestion: Lindeman's Botrytis Riesling,
1998, Coonawarra (Australia)

Menu

West Coast seafood platter
with a dill vinaigrette

This attractive arrangement of fresh and smoked seafoods from the West Coast of Scotland is one of The House of Bruar's very best-sellers. The dressing is best made a week in advance as this allows the flavours to infuse into the oils.

for the seafood

25g smoked scallops

25g Braden Rost (a type of hot smoked salmon)

25g smoked trout

25g smoked mussels

25g gravadlax

25g sherry and rollmop herrings

1 oyster

25g crab, hand picked

25g smoked salmon

25g fresh salmon

for the dill vinaigrette

275ml extra virgin olive oil

275ml groundnut oil

55ml balsamic vinegar

a small bunch of fresh dill

12 black peppercorns, lightly crushed

3 shallots, finely chopped

2 cloves of garlic, crushed

1 bay leaf

1 tsp coarse sea salt

for the accompaniments

fresh leaf salad

soda bread and unsalted butter

For the seafood: Divide the seafood between 4 serving plates and arrange it attractively.

For the dill vinaigrette: Warm both oils together and, while still warming, add all the remaining ingredients and continue to cook the mixture for 2 minutes. Allow the vinaigrette to cool before pouring it into a 725ml bottle. Close the bottle with a cork or screw top and store it in the fridge. Shake the bottle once a day. Before using the vinaigrette, check the seasoning.

To serve, dress the seafood with the dill vinaigrette and present it with a fresh leaf salad and some buttered soda bread.

Chicken and broccoli cheese bake

for the chicken

6 chicken breasts or 1
  whole chicken
1 medium onion, peeled
  and chopped
2 carrots, peeled and
  chopped
2 celery sticks, chopped
a few sprigs of fresh
  parsley
1 fresh bay leaf
a few black peppercorns

for the broccoli

1 large head of broccoli,
  divided into florets
salted water

for the creamy sauce

25ml reserved chicken
  liquor
275ml double cream
50g butter
50g plain flour
salt and freshly ground
  black pepper

for the cheese topping

10g butter
110g breadcrumbs,
  homemade or shop
  bought
50g cheddar cheese,
  grated

for the accompaniments

boiled new potatoes
cooked green beans,
  buttered

For the chicken: Place the chicken breasts or the whole chicken into a large saucepan with the onion, carrots, celery, parsley, bay leaf, peppercorns and enough water to cover everything. Slowly bring the water to the boil, then reduce the heat and simmer until the chicken is cooked – expect this to take about 20 minutes for the chicken breasts or an hour for a whole chicken. Remove the chicken from the pan. Pour the cooking liquid through a strainer, discarding the vegetables, herbs and peppercorns but reserving the liquor. Leave the chicken to cool, then strip the meat off the bones, dice it and set it aside.

For the broccoli: Blanch the broccoli in boiling salted water until just tender. Then drain it and refresh it under cold running water.

For the creamy sauce: Put the reserved cooking liquid into another saucepan and boil it until it is reduced to about 725ml. Add the cream and bring it back to the boil. Make a roux by melting the butter in a small pan and gradually incorporating the flour into it. Cook the butter and flour mixture gently for about 5 minutes. Now whisk the creamy liquid into the roux, a little at a time, to form a thick sauce. Stir the diced chicken and cooked broccoli into the sauce and season to taste with the salt and pepper. Pour this mixture into an ovenproof dish.

For the cheese topping: Preheat the oven to 180°C (gas mark 4). Melt the butter and mix it together with the breadcrumbs and grated cheddar cheese. Spread this over the chicken and broccoli mixture and bake it in the oven for 20 minutes or until brown and bubbling.

Serve with boiled new potatoes and buttered green beans or another green vegetable of your choice.

Cooked vanilla cheesecake
with a fruit coulis

for the sponge base
6 eggs
175g caster sugar,
   flavoured with a
   vanilla pod
175g plain flour
50g unsalted butter,
   melted

for the cheesecake
   topping
225g caster sugar
3 tbsp cornflour
700g full-fat soft cream
   cheese
2 eggs, lightly beaten
1 tsp vanilla essence
300ml whipping cream

for the fruit coulis
275g fresh raspberries
275g fresh strawberries
110g caster sugar
150ml water

for the garnish
a little extra whipping
   cream, whipped

For the sponge base: Preheat the oven to 200°C (gas mark 6). Grease a 25cm round cake tin and dust it with flour. Whisk the eggs and sugar together in a bowl over a pan of hot water. Continue to whisk until the mixture has doubled in volume and is light and creamy. Remove from the heat and continue to whisk until cold and thick. This is called the ribbon stage, as the mixture will trail off the whisk in ribbons when you lift it out of the mixture. Lightly fold in the flour and melted butter. Gently pour the mixture into the prepared tin and bake in the preheated oven for about 30 minutes. The easiest way to test if the sponge is ready is to insert a skewer. The skewer will come out clean when the sponge is cooked. Allow the sponge to cool for 10 minutes in the tin and then turn it out on to a wire rack. When the sponge base has cooled, put it into a buttered loose-bottomed 25cm cake tin.

For the topping: Preheat the oven to 180°C (gas mark 4). Mix the sugar and cornflour together and beat in the cream cheese, making sure everything is incorporated to form a creamy texture. Now beat in the eggs and vanilla essence. Gradually pour in the cream, beating constantly to give a thick, creamy consistency. Pour the mixture over the sponge base and cook in the oven for 45–50 minutes until the top is golden brown. Remove it from the oven and leave it to cool. Allow the cheesecake time to set completely before carefully removing it from the tin.

For the fruit coulis: Blitz 225g of the raspberries, 225g of the strawberries, the caster sugar and the water together. Then gently fold in the remaining fruit.

   To serve, cut the cheesecake into wedges and place a wedge on each plate with a scoop of whipped fresh cream and a pool of the fruit coulis.

Near Strathvaich Forest, Wester Ross

Near Loch of Stenness, Orkney

Café One

Inverness

NORMAN MACDONALD

The premises which are now Café One have been synonymous with good food for as long as I can remember, having previously been the Inverness Wine Bar for many years. For the past three years, Café One has been providing delicious lunches and dinners and the owners, Norman and Karen Macdonald, bring a special warmth and atmosphere to this small restaurant. Norman's love of food gives the menu a creative slant. His skills in the open kitchen, where he cooks for three of the six days that the restaurant is open, give the food its consistently high quality. Norman's chefs, Andrew Strachan and Matthew Urquhart, have worked at Café One for most of the three years of its existence and, together with Norman, they always ensure that, whenever we visit Inverness for the day, we know our trip will be enlivened by lunch at Café One.

Norman says that their success is simply due to his being in the right place at the right time. This is overly modest. Above all else, their success comes from his positive outlook, his ability to work hard and his desire to learn. When he was sixteen, he began his working life as a kitchen porter at the excellent Glenmoriston Hotel. He keenly observed the work of the chef there and left, aged twenty-four, to buy Café One.

Norman believes that his ingredients are everything and he seeks out the best. His wine list is just as excellent as his menus, purchasing it from Irvine Robertson Wines in Leith and Inverarity Vaults. But for Italian wines, he goes to Alivini, from whom he also buys prosciutto, salami and olive oils. Norman uses the best Scottish produce and teams it with ingredients from other countries to produce the mouth-watering food served at Café One. This is food without any pretension, served with care, in an atmosphere that truly represents Highland hospitality.

Norman Macdonald, Proprietor,
with Matthew Urquhart (centre) and Andrew Strachan (right)

CAFÉ ONE

Starter

Fresh tuna and wok-seared vegetables
with Chinese soy, wasabi and pickled ginger

Wine suggestion: A good crisp Gavi Di Gavi from
Piemonte or a Riesling from South Australia

Main course

Tail fillet of Angus beef
with red onion marmalade, olive oil mash
and an oyster mushroom and Marsala jus

Wine suggestion: A Reserve Merlot (Chilean),
Barolo (Italian) or Claret (France)

Dessert

Drambuie-laced hot chocolate fondants

Wine suggestion: Pacherenc du Vic-Bilh, 1999,
Saint-Albert (France) or Vasse Felix Noble Riesling
(Australia)

Menu

Fresh tuna and wok-seared vegetables
with Chinese soy, wasabi and pickled ginger

This is a Café classic – Invernessian sushi, if you like. It has been chosen because, as an effort-equals-award dish, this is fantastic – your dinner party guests will think you have slaved all day when, in actual fact, this will only take twenty minutes, including preparation.

for the wok-seared vegetables
55ml sesame oil (olive oil is fine)
1 small red onion, cut into strips
   lengthways like bean sprouts
1 yellow pepper, chopped into 1cm
   strips
110g shitake mushrooms, chopped into
   1cm wide strips
75g mange tout, cut lengthways like
   the red onion
75g bean sprouts
freshly ground salt and black pepper

for the tuna
55ml olive oil
4 x 110g fresh tuna steaks
freshly ground salt and black pepper

for the accompaniments
60ml good quality Chinese soy such as
   Kikkoman or Pearl River
20g wasabi paste
25g pickled ginger

For the wok-seared vegetables: Heat up a wok, pour in the sesame oil and immediately add the onion, pepper and mushrooms, stirring continuously. As the peppers start to soften, add the mange tout and bean sprouts. Keeping the heat high, continue cooking and stirring for another few minutes and then season the vegetables and remove them from the heat.

For the tuna: Meanwhile pour the olive oil into a hot frying pan or char-grill pan. When the oil is smoking hot, carefully add the tuna (use tongs!), sear for 1 minute, season, turn and sear for a further minute. Remove the tuna from the heat and season the other sides of the steaks.

   To serve, mix the wasabi paste and soy together to make a dressing – use all of the wasabi paste if you like hot food or just a little if you prefer a milder taste. Pour some dressing into 4 small dishes or ramekins and set one on each serving plate. Place a little pickled ginger next to each one – to refresh the taste buds and cleanse the palate. Arrange an equal amount of vegetables in the centre of each plate, place a tuna steak on top and serve at once.

Tail fillet of Angus beef

with red onion marmalade, olive oil mash and an oyster mushroom and Marsala jus

This dish represents good honest Scottish cooking. When you buy your beef, ask your butcher to trim it well and try haggling about the price as fillet tails are not a popular cut and often end up being minced. This should also leave more money to spend on the wine! The marmalade and jus can be made in advance and set aside. If you are doing this, you will need to add a further 275ml of chicken stock to the jus and a glass of red wine to the marmalade when reheating, ensuring both are reduced to the original consistency for serving.

for the red onion marmalade
4 medium red onions, roughly
    chopped
35ml olive oil
75ml balsamic vinegar
75g demerara sugar
125ml red wine
freshly ground salt and black pepper

for the oyster mushroom and
    Marsala jus
450g oyster mushrooms, sliced
8 shallots, finely chopped
35ml olive oil

freshly ground salt and black pepper
175ml Marsala or sweet sherry
570ml chicken stock
8 fresh sage leaves, halved

for the mash
6 large potatoes, peeled
freshly ground salt
75ml extra virgin olive oil, the greener
    the better

for the beef
4 x 225g fillet tails, well-trimmed
a little olive oil, for searing

For the red onion marmalade: On a low heat, gently sauté the red onions in the olive oil for around 20 minutes until soft. Turn up the heat and add the balsamic vinegar, demerara sugar, red wine and seasoning. Let the liquid reduce by half. Then turn the heat back down and stir continuously until the mixture has the same consistency as jam.

For the oyster mushroom and Marsala jus: Sweat the mushrooms and shallots in a large frying pan with the olive oil, salt and pepper. Add the Marsala or sherry and reduce by half. Add the chicken stock and again reduce by half. Add the sage and check the seasoning.

For the mash and beef: Chop the potatoes so that they are all roughly the same size and boil them in a large pan with plenty of salted water for 20–25 minutes. Preheat the oven to 190°C (gas mark 5). Put a char-grill pan or large frying pan on a high heat and add the olive oil. When the oil is smoking, add the beef to the pan and seal on each side until it is dark brown. Place the fillets in an ovenproof dish and put them in the oven for 10 minutes. The potatoes will now be ready so remove the beef from the oven and set it aside to rest while preparing the mash. Drain the potatoes, add the green extra virgin olive oil and mash until the potatoes are creamy.

To serve, place a mound of mash in the centre of each of the 4 serving plates. Slice the beef and fan the slices over the top of the mash. Put a generous spoonful of the red onion marmalade on the side and drizzle the oyster mushroom and Marsala jus around the outside.

Drambuie-laced hot chocolate fondants

150g good quality cooking milk
  chocolate
150g unsalted butter, cut into small
  pieces
60g caster sugar
2 whole eggs
2 egg yolks

30ml Drambuie
20g self-raising flour

for the accompaniment
4 scoops of good quality vanilla ice
  cream
fresh raspberries

Preheat the oven to 190°C (gas mark 5). Melt the chocolate in a bowl that is sitting over a pan of gently simmering water. Once it has melted, gradually add the butter pieces. Whisk the sugar and eggs together and then add the Drambuie. Slowly combine this mixture with the melted butter and chocolate. Sieve the flour into the mixture and gently fold together. Pour the mixture into 4 greased ramekins and bake them in the oven for 8–10 minutes.

To serve, remove the fondants from the ramekins and place one in the centre of each of the 4 serving plates, accompanied by a large scoop of the vanilla ice cream and some raspberries.

MV Hebrides, the Harris ferry

Luskentyre, Isle of Harris

The Ceilidh Place

Ullapool

JEAN URQUHART

The Ceilidh Place epitomises Highland hospitality at its best. The comfortable and elegant hotel is situated on a quiet road in Ullapool, overlooking Loch Broom with the mountains beyond. A row of white-washed houses is the core of the establishment but, across the road and through the garden is the clubhouse – an attractive white building with comfortable but lower priced accommodation.

The Ceilidh Place is not just an extremely cosy and beautifully decorated hotel, it is also an artistic centre with a programme of music (traditional, classical and sometimes jazz) on offer. There are regular art exhibitions as well, and an eclectic bookshop imaginatively stocked. The heart of The Ceilidh Place is the large ground-floor room which offers a food service all day – breakfast to brunch, brunch to lunch and lunch to dinner, with good coffee and home baking that, on tasting, lives up to its mouth-watering appearance. The bar also stocks a fine selection of malt whiskies, and there is a very good wine list as well.

The chef, Michael Lavelle, born and bred in Ullapool, is a Scottish History graduate who has a passion for food, and he has created an enticing menu featuring local fish, shellfish and meat, as well as a truly delicious pudding menu, as high in quality as the first and main courses. So often I find that puddings can be a let-down in restaurants and hotels but this is not the case here. As with the preceding courses, the puddings present a familiar theme with an added twist, for example, Earl Grey and vanilla crème brûlée.

Arguably, the best bit is the upstairs living room with its honesty bar, guests pantry and books to read – warm colours in the décor and walls showing (mostly) the work of Scottish artists. The view from the balcony on a warm summer's morning or a wind-swept winter afternoon makes its own picture show with the extraordinary light of the West Coast. As soon as you enter The Ceilidh Place, the relaxed atmosphere of warmth and welcome envelops you. Jean Urquhart who, with her husband Robert (who died in 1995) created this gem of a place, is a dynamic woman from whom the hotel's unique atmosphere and style emanate.

Michael Lavelle, Head Chef

THE CEILIDH PLACE

Starter

Lentil, cumin and apricot soup

Wine suggestion: Les Meysonniers, 1999, Crozes-
Hermitages Blanc, Chapoutier (France)

Main course

Grilled cod
with garlic mash and rocket purée

Wine suggestion: Capercaillie Chardonnay, 2000
(Australia)

Dessert

Christmas crèmes brûlées

Wine suggestion: The Noble One, 2000,
De Bortoli (Australia)

Menu

Lentil, cumin and apricot soup

We sell a lot of soup during the day at The Ceilidh Place and this one is a very warming combination of flavours. It is also a quick and easy soup to put together.

for the soup
55ml vegetable oil
1 large onion, roughly chopped
3 cloves of garlic, finely diced
1 green chilli, deseeded and finely
   diced
1 small piece of ginger, peeled and
   roughly chopped
2 tbsp freshly ground cumin
1 tbsp freshly ground coriander

1 tbsp garam masala
20 dried apricots
450g red lentils
1 litre vegetable stock (readymade is
   fine)

for the garnish
1 lime
10g fresh mint
10g yoghurt

For the soup: Heat the oil in a large pan, add the onion, garlic, chilli and ginger and fry them for 10 minutes on a low heat. Next add the spices, followed by the apricots and the lentils and fry for a further 5 minutes. After the lentils have absorbed all the oil, add the vegetable stock and bring it to the boil. Simmer the soup for 50 minutes or until the lentils are soft. Now blend or liquidise the soup until it is smooth.

For the garnish: While the soup is simmering, juice the lime, finely shred the fresh mint and add both to the yoghurt.

To serve, after checking the seasoning, pour the soup into 4 bowls and swirl the yoghurt mixture on top.

Grilled cod
with garlic mash and rocket purée

The delicate flavour of a fresh, firm fillet of cod is perfectly set off by the garlic mash and the pepperiness of the rocket purée.

for the rocket purée
50g rocket
100ml extra virgin olive oil
25g walnuts
salt and freshly ground black pepper

for the garlic mash
900g floury potatoes, peeled and cut
  into chunks
50ml double cream

25g unsalted butter
3 cloves of garlic, crushed
salt and freshly ground black pepper

for the grilled cod
salt and freshly ground black pepper
4 x 175g thick fillets of fresh cod
a little olive oil
fennel tops

For the rocket purée: This can be prepared in advance. Put the rocket, olive oil and walnuts in a blender and blend, at high speed, until smooth. Add the seasoning, taste the purée to check that the seasoning is all right and then set it aside.

For the garlic mash: Boil the potatoes in salted water until they are soft. Meanwhile heat the cream until just below boiling point. Drain the potatoes and mash them with the butter. Stir the crushed garlic into the hot cream. Add the garlic cream to the mashed potatoes and combine them thoroughly. Check the seasoning and keep the mash warm, ready for serving.

For the cod: Season the cod fillets on both sides and drizzle a little olive oil over them. Heat the grill to a high temperature, put the fish under it and grill on one side for 6 minutes.

To serve, put some garlic mash in the centre of each of the 4 warmed plates. Place a cod fillet on top, drizzle some rocket purée over the fish and place some fennel tops on each.

Christmas crèmes brûlées

The infusing of the cream with traditional festive spices gives this classic desert a warming wintry flavour.

for the crèmes brûlées

3 large egg yolks

175g caster sugar

275ml double cream

4 cloves

2 cardamom pods

a pinch of ground cinnamon

a pinch of freshly grated nutmeg

1 vanilla pod

a little icing sugar, to finish

For the crèmes brûlées: Put the egg yolks and sugar into a large bowl and whisk them together until pale. Put the cream and the rest of the ingredients, except the icing sugar, into a pan and bring the mixture to just below boiling point. Remove the pan from the heat immediately and allow the mixture to cool. Leave the spices to infuse in the cream for 30 minutes before returning it to a heavy-based pan. Heat the cream mixture up again and, as it comes to the boil, remove it from the heat. Whisk the hot cream into the egg and sugar mixture and combine thoroughly. Next, strain the mixture back into the pan. Reduce the heat and, stirring continuously, allow the mixture to become thick enough to coat the back of a spoon.

Preheat the oven to 170–180°C (gas mark 3–4). Pour the mixture into individual ramekins and put the ramekins in a bain-marie (a high-sided oven tray with enough water to come halfway up the ramekins). Bake the ramekins in the oven for 30 minutes or until the mixture has set. Remove them from the oven and lightly dust the tops with the icing sugar. Put them under a preheated grill and grill at a high temperature until the icing sugar caramelises.

To serve, carefully remove the crèmes brûlées from the ramekins and place one in the centre of each of 4 serving plates.

Glen Shiel

Clifton House

Nairn

J. GORDON MACINTYRE

Gordon Macintyre grew up in Clifton House and he and his wife, Muriel, have now run it as a hotel for fifty years. Despite this, Clifton House is the least hotel-like establishment you could imagine. First impressions are of such a heady mix of flowers, warmth of welcome and what Ianthe Ruthven has described as 'voluptuous clutter' as to remain with one forever. The voluptuous clutter consists of a fascinating mass of antiques, pictures, photographs, furniture, ornaments and flowers – and there are flowers everywhere.

Clifton House is unique in every way and it is simply a treat to be a guest there. Gordon Macintyre is the epitome of a gentle man. I deliberately separate these words to give emphasis to their meaning. He is an actor and, indeed, plays and concerts are performed at Clifton. Gordon loves food and, in his own words, he is terribly, terribly greedy. When he started out he used to call his sister in Forres to ask how to make things like pastry. He is completely self-taught in the kitchen, gradually feeling his way forward, and he eats out inquisitively, always asking about what he has been served so he can reconstruct it himself.

Gordon is passionately selective about his supplies. His lamb comes from Michael Wigan in Sutherland. He has bought fish from Duncan Fraser in Inverness since before the War. His eggs come from Toby Macarthur, who lives locally and supplies the freshest produce. He buys cheeses from Ian Mellis. His butcher is the estimable Michael Gibson at Macbeth's the Butchers in Forres. And the wonderful chickens, cooked to perfection and carved with theatrical aplomb by Gordon in the dining room, come from Mrs Jones from Howtowie, near Inverurie. The puddings at Clifton are a wonderful example of how puddings should be made – the best proper trifle, for example, steeped in sherry.

Absolutely everything at Clifton demonstrates how personalities, such as those of Gordon and Muriel, can put a unique stamp on the very character of an establishment. And the hospitality that radiates from the Macintyres makes any visit to Clifton a sheer joy.

J. Gordon Macintyre, Proprietor, with his son Charles (left)

CLIFTON HOUSE

Starter

Terrine de sarcelle aux pruneaux

Wine suggestion: Quarts de Chaume,
Montbazillac, 1995, or a Sauternes

Main course

Carré d'agneau à la Tourangelle

Wine suggestion: Clos de l'Echo or Clos de la
Dioterie, Chinon

Dessert

Tarte au citron

Wine suggestion: Muscat de Beaumes de
Venise, Chapoutier

Menu

Terrine de sarcelle aux pruneaux

This recipe does involve taking quite a lot of trouble and it requires to be prepared at least three days in advance – but it is well worth it. I suggest using 4 teal but, if teal are not available, use 2 mallard or 2 widgeon. This quantity should make at least three good-sized 1-litre terrines.

for the prunes
225g large prunes, stones removed (the best are Californian prunes – 225g should give you about 9 prunes – or try the big Agen prunes)
275ml dry white wine
40ml light malt whisky, such as Grants or Knockando
150ml port

for the stock
2 pig's trotters, split in half by the butcher
1 onion or 2 large shallots, chopped

4 cloves
4 cloves of garlic, crushed
2 bay leaves
275ml cold water

for the terrine
4 whole teal
sea salt and freshly ground black pepper
1.35kg belly or shoulder pork (this must be of good quality and absolutely free of any gristle and skin)
1 tsp each of pink and green peppercorns
50g pistachio nuts, shelled

40ml light malt whisky, such as Grants or Knockando
150ml port
450g back or streaky bacon, rind removed
3 tbsp fresh parsley, chopped

for the accompaniments
green salad leaves or watercress
pickled walnuts or gherkins
gooseberry conserve (readymade is fine)

For the prunes: Start by soaking the stoned prunes overnight in the white wine, whisky and port.

For the teal or mallard: Preheat the oven to 220°C (gas mark 7). Pluck and draw the birds – or you could ask your butcher or poulterer to do this for you. Separate the flesh from the skin and bones, remove any pieces of shot and reserve the livers. Put the carcasses on a tray in the hot oven for half an hour. Remove the carcasses from the oven, allow them to cool and take off any remaining flesh. It is important, however, to be very selective in this and to use only tender meat, avoiding any gristly bits and making sure there is no shot lurking in the flesh. Chop the breast and leg meat up into small pieces.

For the stock: Put the trotters, onion, cloves, garlic and bay leaves into a pan with the cold water and put them on to simmer. The longer you leave the stock cooking, the better it will be. Skim off any froth that forms on the top and add more cold water if necessary. You should end up with about 300ml. Strain the stock, cover it and refrigerate.

For the terrine: The day after making the stock, remove the cut-up duck flesh and the pork from the fridge. In one bowl put small select cubes or slivers of duck and the best inside pieces of pork or really good bits of pork fat. To this add the best of the duck livers (no green bits), plus the pistachio nuts and the pink and green peppercorns. Put the remaining cut-up duck and pork, plus anything rescued from the carcasses cooked in the oven, through a robo coupe or food processor and place the minced meat in a separate bowl. Divide the whisky and port between the two. Cover and refrigerate for 24 hours.

For each terrine, take a piece of kitchen foil about 50cm x 50cm, fold it several times to form a ribbon about 3cm in width, making sure the edges are folded in, and place it lengthwise down each terrine dish. This is used to support the terrine as you draw it out of its container. Carefully put a layer of cling film on top of the kitchen foil ribbon, leaving a good overhang. Line each dish with a layer of bacon. Put the contents of both bowls, as well as the prunes and the liquid used for soaking them, and the parsley into the stock and mix everything together thoroughly.

Pack the mixture in layers. If you used whole birds, you could stretch the skins tightly across the terrine to form a protective top layer. Fold over the cling film. Cover with the lid or kitchen foil and cook at 180°C (gas mark 4) in a bain-marie in the oven for $1^{1}/_{2}$–2 hours. Allow the terrines to cool and then refrigerate them for at least 24 hours. This will give them time to firm up and mature. They will keep perfectly for a week and they freeze well.

To serve, slice across the grain to get the full effect of the pattern. Garnish with a tiny green salad or some watercress, a few pickled walnuts or gherkins and some gooseberry conserve.

Carré d'agneau à la Tourangelle

You will need to start this dish at least two days in advance of serving as the lamb has to be marinated for a minimum of two days. Here at Clifton House I use racks of lamb from either Michael Gibson or Sir Michael Wigan of North Highland Fine Lamb. Both supply small lambs that are quite perfect.

for the marinade
400ml dry white wine
1 red onion, chopped
juice of 1 lemon
sea salt and freshly ground black
    pepper

for the lamb
4 racks of lamb
4 tbsp light honey (e.g. clover)
1 tbsp fresh rosemary, chopped
16 Victoria plums

for the accompaniment
green salad leaves

For the marinade: Mix all the ingredients together in a large bowl.

For the lamb: First trim off the outer fine skin, if this has not been done already, and put it into the marinade. Then add the racks of lamb, which I usually leave to marinate for at least two days.

On the day of cooking, line a tray with two layers of foil (this should save a lot of work for the washer-up as the honey burns). Place the racks on the tray, skin side up, and drizzle all over with honey. Then sprinkle liberally with the rosemary. The salt and pepper in the marinade will be sufficient so there is no need to add more at this stage.

Preheat the oven at 200°C (gas mark 6) and sear the lamb for 5 minutes. Then turn the oven down to 180°C (gas mark 4) for 20 minutes. Take out the tray, add the plums and return to the oven for a further 5 minutes. This will be enough time to heat the plums through without causing them to burst. The honey burns off and the plums give a wonderful sharpness.

To serve, place paper frills on the top bones, present the dish and carve straight down into the cutlets.

Tarte au citron

for the case
250g plain flour
200g unsalted butter
100g caster sugar
2 egg yolks
1 tsp water (optional)

for the filling
300ml double cream
zest and juice of 4–5 lemons
6 eggs
200g caster sugar

For the case: Preheat the oven to 180°C (gas mark 4). Beat the sugar and butter together until white and fluffy. Blend in the egg yolks and then work in the flour, adding the water if necessary. Roll the pastry out and line the flan case with it. The flan case I use is 4cm deep and 30cm in diameter. Leave the pastry to rest in the fridge for 15 minutes before baking blind for 30 minutes. To do this, line the pastry with greaseproof paper and put ceramic baking beans or dried beans on top of it. The beans will ensure that the base of the flan does not rise and will prevent the sides from collapsing.

For the filling: Beat the cream very lightly, add the rest of the ingredients, mix everything together and put the filling into the case. Lower the oven temperature to 70°C and return the flan to the oven for about 30 minutes.

Serve at room temperature with some vanilla syrup or pouring cream, and perhaps some raspberries to garnish.

Corriegour Lodge Hotel

Loch Lochy, by Spean Bridge
CHRISTIAN AND IAN DREW

Ian and Christian Drew have owned and run Corriegour Lodge for six years. A hunting lodge dating from Victorian times, Corriegour is a gleaming white house which sits high above the A82 road. With its panoramic views down the Great Glen and across Loch Lochy, it must be one of the most beautifully located hotels in the Highlands. Within the grounds of Corriegour are pretty gardens which include a waterfall and a small lochside beach with a jetty.

Ian is responsible for the reputation of the food in the Loch View restaurant and the breakfasts and dinners provide some of the best food to be eaten in Scotland, never mind the Highlands. He constantly seeks the very best produce available. As with all the best places to eat, Ian shows great loyalty to his suppliers. He buys meat from Stewart Grant, the butcher in Dornoch, and his game comes from Lochaber Game. He buys hares and rabbits from the surrounding estates. Robert Milne of Peterhead supplies all the white fish used in the kitchen at Corriegour. And his shellfish – scallops, crab and langoustines – comes from Isle of Skye Seafoods, while the prawns and queen scallops are obtained from the Fishy Business in Kyle of Lochalsh. Yoghurt and cheese come from the West Highland dairies at Achmore, near Plockton, and the fruit and vegetables are supplied (and delivered!) by Donnie Macleod of Ardesier, who also supplies Ian with organic lamb. Ian is faithful to his excellent wine supplier, Peter Henderson, of Edinburgh.

A self-taught cook, Ian cooks from instinct and is singularly unimpressed by pretension. He trained to be an actor and he maintains that cooking is just a different art form. The Drews' roots are in the Highlands – Christian's grandfather was a gamekeeper on the Knoydart estates. And the atmosphere at Corriegour is one of great welcome and warmth, reflecting their Highland origins. Log fires burn in the two sitting rooms and the general ambience is of great conviviality. Truly, Corriegour encapsulates the essence of a Highland hotel – the very best food and a genuine warmth of welcome.

Ian Drew, Proprietor and Head Chef

CORRIEGOUR LODGE HOTEL

Starter

Roast breast of squab pigeon
with foie gras, on a bed of green lentils and
served with a thyme jus

Wine suggestion: Chinon Rouge, Château de Ligré,
2–3 years old, Pierre Ferrand, Loire (France)

Main course

Roast loin of wild venison
on a pearl barley risotto with celeriac purée
and a blueberry and game gravy

Wine suggestion: Hunter Valley Shiraz,
3–4 years old, Capercaillie (Australia) or
Châteauneuf-du-Pape, Barbe Rac, 6–8 years old,
Selection Parcellaire, Chapoutier (France)

Dessert

Assiette of strawberry puddings

Wine suggestion: Muscat de Rivesaltes,
2–3 years old, Chapoutier (France), De Casta Rosado,
Rosé, 1–2 years old, Miguel Torres (Spain) or Bollinger
Grande Année Rosé, Champagne (France) – for
special occasions!

Menu

Roast breast of squab pigeon

with foie gras, on a bed of green lentils and served with a thyme jus

for the green lentils
1 onion, diced
a small knob of unsalted butter
100g bacon lardons
2 fresh bay leaves
2 sprigs of fresh rosemary
250g green lentils, soaked for around 2
   hours and drained
salt and freshly ground black pepper

for the thyme jus
4 shallots, peeled and minced
70g unsalted butter

200ml port
3 sprigs of fresh thyme
1 litre good chicken stock
200ml veal stock
salt and freshly ground black pepper

for the pigeon breasts
2 squab pigeons, breasts removed
salt and freshly ground black pepper
15ml olive oil

for the foie gras
4 x 50g pieces of grade A foie gras

For the green lentils: Sauté the onion in the butter with the bacon lardons. Add the bay leaves, rosemary, green lentils, salt and pepper, cover with water and cook for about 25 minutes until the lentils are soft. Check the seasoning.

For the thyme jus: Sweat the shallots in 45g of the butter until they are translucent and then add the port and thyme. Reduce the sauce over a medium heat until it becomes syrupy and almost all of it has evaporated. Add the two stocks and the salt and pepper and continue cooking until it has reduced by about three-quarters. Now strain the sauce through muslin and check the seasoning. Finally whisk in the remaining 25g of the butter to give the sauce a glaze.

For the pigeon breasts: Preheat the oven to 180°C (gas mark 4). Season the 4 pigeon breasts and seal them, skin side down, in the olive oil in a hot ovenproof pan for 3 minutes until the skin is nicely browned. Turn them over and brown them on the other side for 1 minute. Transfer the breasts to the oven and roast them for 4 minutes. Remove them and leave them to rest in a warm place for 4 minutes.

For the foie gras: In a very hot dry pan, sear the foie gras for 1 minute on each side. Pour off the excess fat (it can be kept and used for another dish such as sautéing potatoes). Put the cooked foie gras on kitchen paper and keep it warm until you are ready to serve.

To serve, place a mound of green lentils in the centre of each of the 4 serving plates, with the foie gras on top of it. Slice each pigeon breast across the middle and fan the slices out over the foie gras. Drizzle over the thyme jus and serve immediately.

Roast loin of wild venison

on a pearl barley risotto with celeriac purée and a blueberry and game gravy

for the pearl barley risotto

45ml olive oil

2 leeks, finely chopped

4 shallots, peeled and finely chopped

200g pearl barley

100g semi-dried raisins

50g pine nuts

salt and freshly ground black pepper

15g dried morel mushrooms, soaked in
   100ml boiling water for about 30
   minutes

500ml chicken stock (readymade is
   fine)

400ml rich red wine

for the blueberry and game gravy

50ml vegetable oil

700g venison trimmings

2 carrots, finely chopped

1 onion, peeled and finely chopped

3 cloves of garlic, crushed

1 bay leaf (fresh or dried)

3 sprigs of fresh thyme

5mg black peppercorns, crushed

1.75 litre brown chicken or beef stock

500ml Merlot wine

1 x 225g punnet of fresh blueberries

for the celeriac purée

1 large celeriac, peeled and cut into
   chunks

about 500ml milk

30g unsalted butter

salt and freshly ground black pepper

for the roast loin of wild venison

1x 600g loin of wild venison

salt and freshly ground black pepper

a little olive oil, for searing

for the accompaniments

4 portions of dauphinois potatoes

For the pearl barley risotto: Heat the olive oil in a pan over a medium heat. Stir in the leeks and shallots and fry them until they begin to colour. Rinse off the pearl barley, add it to the leeks and shallots and fry it until it starts to turn a nut-brown colour. Add the raisins, pine nuts and seasoning and cook for 5 minutes. Now add the mushrooms, their soaking liquid, wine and stock, turn the heat down to very low and allow it to cook until all the liquid has been absorbed. The pearl barley should be soft but still retain a little bite.

For the blueberry and game gravy: Heat the vegetable oil in a large saucepan over a moderate heat and, working in batches, brown the venison trimmings and transfer them to a bowl. (If you put too many pieces in the pan at once, they will

steam and will never brown.) Reduce the heat and, in the same pan, cook the vegetables until they are nicely browned. Return the venison trimmings to the pan, along with the garlic, bay leaf, thyme and peppercorns, add the stock and wine and cook at a rolling simmer for about 1 hour, skimming the surface every 15 minutes. When the gravy has reduced to about 500ml, strain it through a fine sieve. Now return it to the pan and reduce it again until you have about 200ml of plum-coloured sauce. Check the seasoning and add the blueberries to the pan, stirring well to ensure they are all coated. Keep the gravy warm on a very low heat until you are ready to serve.

For the celeriac purée: Put the celeriac chunks into a pan with enough milk to cover them, then cook them over a moderate heat until soft. Drain them and put them in a food processor or blender. When smooth, return the celeriac purée to the pan and, over a low heat, cook it until it thickens, allowing as much moisture as possible to evaporate. Now beat in the butter and seasoning.

For the roast loin of wild venison: Preheat the oven to 200°C (gas mark 6). Season the venison all over. Put the olive oil into a pan over a high heat and sear the venison on all sides until it is nicely coloured. Transfer it to a roasting pan and put it in the oven for 8–10 minutes. Remove it again from the oven and then leave it to rest in a warm place, for around 5 minutes, before cutting it into slices.

To serve, spoon a mound of pearl barley risotto on to the center of each of the 4 serving plates and put some celeriac purée next to it. Arrange the sliced venison on top and drizzle the blueberry and game gravy around the outside of the mound of risotto, ensuring that the blueberries are evenly distributed between the plates. Present the dish with the dauphinois potatoes.

Assiette of strawberry puddings

for the mascarpone sorbet
250g mascarpone cheese
150ml stock syrup

for the meringues
4 egg whites
a pinch of cream of tartar
150g caster sugar
1 tsp vanilla extract

for the jelly
150ml stock syrup
50ml pink champagne

100ml sweet white wine (Sauternes or
    Muscat would be ideal)
2 leaves of gelatin, soaked in cold
    water until soft
10 strawberries, sliced

for the parfait
125g caster sugar
125ml water
4 egg yolks
250ml strawberry purée (readymade is
    fine)
500ml double cream

For the mascarpone sorbet: Put the mascarpone cheese and the stock syrup into a bowl and mix them together with a spoon. Transfer the mixture to an ice-cream machine and churn it until smooth. If you don't have an ice-cream machine, put the mixture into a large plastic or Tupperware container and place it in the freezer. Every hour, mix it with a fork. When it is frozen and set around the edges, transfer the mixture to a mixer and blend it until smooth. Now put it back in the freezer and leave it until it is set.

For the meringue: Preheat the oven to 140°C (gas mark 1). In a mixer on a low speed, beat the egg whites until they become frothy. Add the cream of tartar and turn the speed up to high, adding the sugar in a steady flow and beating until the mixture is thick and glossy. Remove this from the mixer and gently fold in the vanilla extract. Line a baking tray with some baking parchment and, using one of the parfait moulds used later in this recipe as a template, draw round it 4 times to give 4 circles on the baking parchment. Put the meringue mixture into a piping bag fitted with a 15mm star-shaped nozzle and pipe little crowns of meringue over the circles on the parchment. Bake the crowns of meringue from between 1 hour 25 minutes and 1 hour 30 minutes until they are crisp and dry but still a little chewy in the middle.

For the jelly: Mix the stock syrup, champagne and sweet white wine together. Drain the cold water from the gelatin and put the leaves in a small pan with enough of the stock syrup mixture to cover it. Heat until the gelatin is melted and then add the rest of the stock syrup mixture. Put the sliced strawberries into 4 individual jelly moulds to form a fan shape and pour the gelatin liquid over them. Put the moulds in the fridge for 4 hours to set.

For the parfait: Put the sugar in a pan, cover it with the water and bring to it the boil. Continue cooking at a high heat for about 5 minutes until the mixture reaches the soft-ball stage (118°C on a sugar thermometer). Whisk the egg yolks in a food mixer until they are white and then slowly pour the sugar over them. Continue whisking the egg and sugar mixture until it has become cool and stiff. Fold in the strawberry purée. Whisk the cream to the stage where it forms soft peaks, gently fold it into the mixture, pour the parfait into four 50ml moulds and freeze them.

To serve, run the metal sides of the jelly moulds under hot water very briefly and turn the jellies out on to the 4 serving plates. Remove the parfaits from the freezer and warm the moulds in your hands. Upturn the moulds so that the parfaits slide out on to the serving plates. Put a crown of meringue on top of each parfait and flash them under a hot grill or with a blow torch until lightly browned. Place a scoop of the mascapone sorbet next to each one. Dust the plates with icing sugar and drizzle some strawberry purée around the outside.

Allasdale beach, Barra

The Creel Restaurant

St Margaret's Hope, Orkney

ALAN CRAIGIE

The recommendations for The Creel came to us from far and wide – literally. But until our visit to see for ourselves and to experience just what makes this restaurant so special, we had never been to Orkney.

And we were certainly not disappointed! For a start, for any first-time visitors to Orkney be prepared for lush and cultivated islands which make up for being almost tree-less in the sheer number of their cattle, their wild beauty and their bird life that can be seen and heard. The beaches and the architecture of the villages and small towns dotted throughout are just stunning and St Margaret's Hope is a most attractive little fishing town. The Creel is right on the front, and the fairly small restaurant is both comfortable and spacious, and decorated beautifully to complement its position on the sea bay.

Alan and Joyce Craigie have owned and run The Creel for seventeen years. Both Orcadians, they have lived and worked in California – Alan was chef at the British Consul in Los Angeles before coming back, and he is a chef of great skill. The menu is simply mouth-watering.

The produce Alan uses is the best – as is the case with every other establishment in this book. He buys fish from the fish market in Scrabster – strange as it may seem, there is no fish market in Orkney. The shellfish comes from the bay right in front of the restaurant, he buys island meat from the butcher in Kirkwall, and uses fruit and vegetables in season from local growers. As well as buying cheeses from local cheese-makers, he has others sent from Ian Mellis. The bannocks, like everything else, are homemade – there are two types, one a plain flour bannock, the other made with beremeal, a sort of barley grain from Orkney – and especially noteworthy are the chocolates served with coffee after dinner.

All the food is as memorably delicious as the many reports to us on The Creel's excellence testified. And you can stay there, too, for The Creel is a restaurant with a few rooms. But what makes The Creel so special is the genuine warmth of welcome and the efficient yet homely service. I can't wait to go back!

THE CREEL RESTAURANT

Starter

Brandade of salt ling

Wine suggestion: Alsace Grand Cru, 1996,
Riesling, Steinert (France)

Main course

Dived scallops with avocado and
pink grapefruit salsa and a
yellow pepper dressing

Wine suggestion: Cloudy Bay Sauvignon Blanc,
2000 (New Zealand)

Dessert

Baked glazed lemon tart

Wine suggestion: Botrytis Semillon Sauternes,
1998, Peter Lehmann, Barossa (Australia)

Menu

Brandade of salt ling

This is how we serve brandade, a type of fish pâté, at The Creel – a firm favourite of my son since he was small. If you are salting the ling yourself for this recipe, you need to start it 2 days before cooking.

for the salt ling
450g fresh ling (cod is also fine)
1kg coarse sea salt

15ml double cream
1 dsp fresh chives, chopped
1 dsp fresh parsley, chopped

for the other ingredients
175g smoked salmon, sliced
2 tbsp olive oil
50g shallot, chopped
1 clove of garlic, crushed
55ml white wine

for the garnish
some mixed salad leaves
4 servings of mayonnaise (readymade
   is fine)
lemon wedges

For the salt ling: Cover the bottom of a plastic container with sea salt. Set the ling on the salt and completely cover it with more salt. Place the container in the fridge, leave it there for 24 hours and then wash off the salt with plenty of cold water. Fill a large container with fresh cold water and soak the ling in this in the fridge for a further 24 hours. The ling is now ready to cook. (If you prefer to miss out this step you can buy salt fish from any good fishmonger.)

For the brandade: Line a terrine dish with cling film. Reserve a little smoked salmon for decorating the top of the terrine. Put the rest of the smoked salmon in a layer over the cling film, ensuring that there is enough of an overhang to allow you to fold it over the top of the filled terrine and cover it. Put the salt ling in fresh cold water, bring it to the boil and poach it for about 10 minutes. Heat half of the olive oil in a small saucepan and cook the shallots and garlic very gently, until they are soft and translucent. When softened, add the wine and cook for a further 4–5 minutes. Put the cooked garlic, shallots and wine mixture into a food processor and blend it until it is smooth. Now add the ling and blend everything again until you have a smooth consistency. Put the cream and the remaining olive oil into a pan, bring them to the boil and then remove the pan from the heat. Stir the cream and olive oil mixture into the ling mixture and add the chives and parsley. Fill the terrine with this mixture and carefully fold the smoked salmon over the top so that the ling mixture is completely covered. If you serve this dish immediately it will still be warm, but it can also be chilled and served cold.

To serve, cut good thick slices of the brandade and lay them on a bed of salad leaves. Garnish with the reserved salmon and lemon wedges. We would serve this with our own homemade mayonnaise but there are many very good readymade mayonnaises available to buy.

Dived scallops

with avocado and pink grapefruit salsa and a
yellow pepper dressing

Scallops are my favourite shellfish. Nothing could be better than scallops delivered
at 6.00 p.m. – just one hour before the restaurant opens – by the diver who has
caught them that afternoon. They are then carefully opened and served – so fresh
and simple. The avocado and pink grapefruit salsa and the yellow pepper dressing
can be made in advance and refrigerated until needed.

for the avocado and
   pink grapefruit salsa
2 ripe avocados, peeled
   and finely diced
2 pink grapefruit, peeled,
   segmented and finely
   diced
25g fresh coriander,
   finely chopped
1 fresh red chilli, deseeded and finely chopped

2 spring onions, finely
   chopped
10g fresh chives,
   chopped
juice of 2 limes

**for the yellow pepper
   dressing**
2 yellow peppers
a little olive oil
5ml Dijon mustard

10g fresh parsley,
   chopped
juice of $1/2$ a lemon

for the scallops
24 small hand-dived
   scallops (6 per person)
75ml olive oil

For the avocado and pink grapefruit salsa: Mix all the ingredients together in a
plastic bowl, cover with cling film and refrigerate for at least 15 minutes.

For the yellow pepper dressing: Preheat the oven to 190° (gas mark 5). Put the
whole peppers on an oven tray, sprinkle them with a little olive oil and roast them
in the oven for 25 minutes. Remove the peppers from the oven and cover them
with cling film – this will make removing the skins easier. When the peppers are
cool, remove the skins and seeds and place the flesh in a blender. Add the
remaining ingredients and blend everything together to make a smooth dressing.

For the scallops: Warm a little olive oil in a non-stick pan. Add the scallops and
cook gently for 2 minutes only on each side – depending on the size of the pan,
you may need to do this in batches.

To serve, drizzle the yellow pepper dressing round the edges of 4 serving plates,
place some salsa in the centre and arrange the cooked scallops evenly around this.

Baked glazed lemon tart

I have included a lemon tart because it is one of the classic sweets – its sharp refreshing taste is a great way to finish a meal.

for the pastry	for the filling	a little icing sugar, for
275g plain flour	3 medium lemons	dusting
50g icing sugar	300ml eggs (about 6,	
150g butter	depending on size)	
1 small egg	275g caster sugar	
2 drops of vanilla essence	275ml double cream	

For the pastry: Preheat the oven to 180°C (gas mark 4). You will need a loose-bottomed flan tin that is about 20cm in diameter and 5cm deep. Put the flour, icing sugar and butter in a food processor with the double blade fitted. Turn it on to a slow speed and, after about a minute, the mixture will begin to resemble breadcrumbs. (If you do not have a food processor, rub the butter into the flour using the tips of your fingers until the breadcrumb stage is reached. Then mix in the icing sugar.) Now add the egg and vanilla essence and continue to mix until the pastry just begins to form. (Use a spatula for this stage if you are not using a food processor.) Remove the pastry from the processor or bowl, place it on a lightly floured worktop and form it into a neat round, flat shape. Cover it with cling film and refrigerate for at least 25 minutes.

Remove the pastry from the fridge, reserve a small piece of it and roll out the remainder on a lightly floured worktop, until it is slightly bigger than the flan tin. Carefully place the pastry into the flan case, ensuring that there is a good 1cm of an overhang. Do not cut this off. Line the case with greaseproof paper, fill it with ceramic baking beans (dried beans or pasta shapes will work just as well) and bake blind in the oven for 10 minutes. Baking blind will stop the pastry base rising and will also prevent the sides of the tart from collapsing. Remove the beans and greaseproof paper and return the flan case to the oven for a further 5–10 minutes to finish cooking the pastry. If any cracks appear in the flan case after cooking, carefully fill them with some of the reserved dampened raw pastry.

For the filling: First grate the lemons on the fine side of a grater and then juice them. Whisk the eggs and sugar together and then stir in the lemon zest and juice.

Gently fold in the cream. Reduce the oven temperature to 140°C (gas mark 1). Take a sheet of tinfoil at least as long as the circumference of the flan tin and four times as deep. Fold the tinfoil into four pleats, so that it is the same depth as the tin, and secure it around the outside of the tin – this will protect the mixture while cooking. Pour the cold filling into the flan case while the case is still warm to help to seal the mixture into the case. For the proposed tin size, bake for 1 hour 20 minutes or until the filling feels set. (Reduce the cooking time to as short as 45 minutes if you are using a much shallower tin.)

To serve, allow the tart to cool, then trim off and discard the excess pastry and remove the tart from the tin. Preheat the grill or a blowtorch if you have one. Cut the tart into good-sized portions, sieve a little icing sugar over the top and caramelise the sugar under the grill or with the blowtorch. You can serve this with cream or ice cream but it is just as delicious on its own.

Loch Melfort, Argyll

The Cross

Kingussie
TONY AND RUTH HADLEY

Tony and Ruth Hadley ran The Cross as a restaurant in the main street of this pretty little Highland village, just off the main A9 road, for nine years before they bought an old tweed mill up the hill from the main street and converted it, mostly to Tony's design, into a nine-bedroom hotel, with the restaurant on the ground floor. On arrival, the warmth of welcome from Tony, a Yorkshireman, sets the scene for the heart-warming experience of staying and eating at The Cross. I once met a single lady staying here who told me the next morning that she had felt immediately at home, and that Tony's gentle courteousness, combined with his humour, had erased all the potential self-consciousness experienced by many when travelling alone.

The food is quite simply wonderful. Ruth Hadley is a self-taught chef with an eye for details of taste, presentation and quality which makes eating at The Cross such a treat. There is no choice on the menu until the main course, when a choice of two dishes is offered, and again at the pudding course. The cheeses deserve particular mention. A choice of six are arranged on a plate and Tony tells you not only what each is but gives advice on the order in which they should be eaten for their best appreciation.

As for the wines, well, Tony chooses six – three white, three red – from his extensive list of 350 wines to go with each evening's menu, none of which come from France. He buys no French wine for two reasons – because he doesn't believe they offer value for money and also because he disagrees with government policies in France.

Breakfast, for those who stay, consists of fresh fruit, organic yoghurt and the best croissants made anywhere in the world, with toasted granary bread and three jams or jellies which might include, for instance, organic strawberry jam, pear and rosemary jelly and lemon and Earl Grey marmalade. Dinner at The Cross is so perfectly balanced in the composition of the menu that finding room for this perfect breakfast the next morning is never a problem. It is no wonder that so very many of the guests at The Cross – either for dinner or as hotel guests – are on return visits.

Ruth Hadley, Proprietor (right) with Becca Henderson

THE CROSS

Starter

Langoustines and avocados
with pesto

Wine suggestion: Sauvignon Blanc, 2000,
Groenkloof, Neil Ellis, Stellenbosch
(South Africa)

Main course

Pan-fried halibut
with a red pepper and orange sauce

Wine suggestion: Soave Classico Superiore DOC,
1998, Foscarino, Stefano Inama (Italy)

Dessert

Chocoholic's delight

Wine suggestion: Moscatel de Valencia DO,
2001, Vicente Gandía (Spain)

Langoustines and avocados
with pesto

for the avocados
juice of $1/2$ a lime
1 tsp caster sugar
$1/2$ tsp salt
3 medium or 2 large
   avocados, peeled and
   de-stoned
6 sprigs of fresh mint,
   chopped
6 sprigs of fresh basil,
   chopped

6 fresh chives, snipped

for the pesto
1 handful of fresh basil
   leaves
1 tbsp pine nuts
25g Parmesan cheese,
   grated
125ml olive oil
salt and freshly ground
   black pepper

for the langoustines
12 or 16 fresh
   langoustines (220g
   fresh or frozen prawns
   are also fine)

for the garnish
2 tomatoes, skinned,
   deseeded and chopped

For the avocados: Put the lime juice into a bowl, add the sugar and salt and stir to dissolve. Mash the avocado flesh with a fork or chop it finely, then add it to the bowl along with the herbs and stir everything together. Cover the mixture in the bowl with cling film, making sure that no air is in contact with the mixture or it will become discoloured. You can prepare this up to 2 hours in advance and store it in the fridge.

For the pesto: Simply blitz the basil, pine nuts and Parmesan in a food processor, gradually adding the olive oil as you go, and then season it to taste.

For the langoustines: If you are using fresh langoustines cook them for 3–4 minutes in a large pan of boiling water. Remove them from the boiling water and plunge them into cold water to stop them from overcooking. Now drain the langoustines and, when they are cool, shell them, taking care to remove the black thread of intestine running along the back. If using frozen prawns, allow enough time for them to defrost fully before serving.

   To serve, put some of the avocado mixture in the centre of each plate and drizzle some pesto around it. Evenly space the langoustines or prawns round the plate and finally garnish with the chopped tomato.

Pan-fried halibut

with a red pepper and orange sauce

In this dish, the contrast in colour between the bright reddish orange of the sauce and the vivid green of the vegetables is quite stunning.

for the red pepper and orange sauce
3 red peppers, chopped and deseeded
300ml freshly squeezed orange juice
  (not concentrate)
1/2 tbsp caster sugar
1 tsp wine vinegar

for the halibut
4 portions of halibut

salt and freshly ground black pepper
25g plain flour
a little light oil, for frying

for the vegetables
1/2 savoy cabbage, chopped
1 large leek, chopped
25g unsalted butter
salt and freshly ground black pepper

For the red pepper and orange sauce: Put the chopped peppers into a food processor, add 200ml of the orange juice and blend. Strain the mixture through a sieve into a pan and add the sugar and vinegar. Place the pan over a low heat and slowly reduce it to approximately half the original quantity.

For the pan-fried halibut: Season and lightly flour the fish portions. Heat the oil in a large frying pan and cook the fish for just 3–4 minutes on each side.

For the vegetables: While the fish is cooking, lightly sautée the chopped vegetables in the butter and season them to taste.

When ready to serve, add the remaining orange juice to the sauce and reheat it. Arrange a bed of sautéed vegetables on each of the 4 serving plates, place a cooked halibut portion on top and surround this with the sauce.

Chocoholic's delight

250g dark chocolate (at least 70% cocoa solids)

4 large eggs, yolks and whites separated

110g sugar

3 tbsp warm water

1 tbsp Drambuie

for the accompaniments

4 portions of seasonal soft fruit

4 scoops of vanilla ice cream (or another flavour of your choice)

Preheat the oven to 180°C (gas mark 4). Grease the bottom of a 20cm loose-bottomed cake tin with a little butter and then line it with greaseproof paper. Melt the chocolate carefully – either in a bowl over hot water or in a microwave – and then set it aside. Put the egg yolks and sugar into a bowl and whisk them together until the mixture is light and fluffy. Next, stir in the melted chocolate, followed by the warm water and the Drambuie. In another bowl, whisk the egg whites until they form soft peaks. Stir a third of the whisked egg whites into the chocolate mixture and then carefully fold in the remainder. Pour the mousse mixture into the greased cake tin and bake it for 15 minutes. Take it out of the oven, leave it to cool and chill in the fridge for at least 2 hours – but do remember to remove the mousse cake from the fridge about half an hour before serving.

To serve, cut the mousse cake into thick wedges – if you use a hot, wet knife, this will prevent the cake sticking to the knife and give nice clean edges. Place a wedge of cake on each of the 4 serving plates, along with some of the seasonal soft fruit – even a coulis of your choice – and a scoop of ice cream.

Barra

Near Kylesku, Sutherland

Kylesku jetty, Sutherland

The Dower House
Muir of Ord
ROBYN AND MENA AITCHISON

Situated a mile outside the village of Muir of Ord, The Dower House is a small hotel lived in and run for the past fifteen years by Robyn and Mena Aitchison. As you turn off the main road through maroon painted gates, the driveway leads you through a most lovely garden in which many of the trees and shrubs were planted some two hundred years ago when The Dower House was built. It is a single-storey building of great architectural eccentricity – the sort of *cottage orné* gem only found in Scotland. Inside, the colours are warm and vibrant and the furnishings are antique, exquisite and deeply interesting. There are five, beautifully appointed bedrooms.

The Aitchisons love the fascinating mix of guests who come to them from all over the world, as well as the many who live locally and regularly dine at The Dower House. Robyn is the cook. He is warm and genial and loves eating as well as cooking. He constantly sources the best ingredients, buying as much organic produce as he can as well as using local produce, most notably beef, lamb, venison and soft fruits in their season. He mainly buys his fish from Duncan Fraser in Inverness, and his cheeses come from the excellent Ian Mellis.

Robyn gets his culinary inspiration from his own imagination, and the large number of guests who return, year after year, is a testament to his success. With the tasteful combination of style and cosiness, the mass of flowers, books and fascinating *objets d'art* to admire and intrigue, the delicious food and warmth of welcome, Robyn and Mena are contributing greatly to the reputation of Highland hospitality.

THE DOWER HOUSE

Starter

Chilled grilled red gurnard
with sautéed cod roe and a chilli dressing

Wine suggestion: a chilled Saumur-Champigny

Main course

Pan-fried wood pigeon
on a bed of wild mushroom risotto

Wine suggestion: Pinot Noir, 2000, Felton Road,
Otago (New Zealand)

Dessert

Lemon tart
with white rum

Wine suggestion: a Monbazillac or
Sauternes (France)

Menu

Chilled grilled red gurnard
with sautéed cod roe and a chilli dressing

Red gurnard is a cheap, tasty and under-utilized fish from the waters around the British Isles and is a really good alternative to red mullet. Cod roe, although only available for a short season, can be bought and frozen, to be used at any time of the year as a delicious snack or as part of a seafood dish. You can buy cod roe fresh and poach it yourself or purchase it already poached from the fishmonger.

The combination of the warm roe and the cold gurnard with the tangy chilli dressing is delicious. As well as the cooking times, you should allow 2 hours' marinating time for this dish.

for the chilli marinade/dressing
5 tbsp virgin olive oil
juice of 2 limes
8 large fresh basil leaves, thinly sliced
3 small dried chilli peppers, crushed
Maldon sea salt and fresh coarsely
  ground black pepper

for the fish and red pepper
2 tbsp olive oil
4 red gurnard fillets
1 red pepper, deseeded and thinly
  sliced into rings

for the cod roe
1 tbsp olive oil
4 slices of a large poached cod roe (if
  the roe is small, 8 slices)

for the garnish
1 tbsp of salted capers
a small handful of fresh basil leaves
fresh fennel

For the chilli marinade/dressing: Put the olive oil, lime juice, basil leaves, chilli peppers, salt and pepper in a bowl and combine them using a whisk. Put the mixture aside for half an hour to allow the flavours to infuse before pouring it through a strainer.

For the fish and red pepper: Lightly oil the fillets and grill them, skin side down, for 2 minutes. Turn the fillets and grill them for a further 2 minutes or until the skin is brown and crisp. Allow the fish to cool and then remove any bones with tweezers. In a frying pan, add a small amount of oil, turn the heat up high and quickly brown the rings of red pepper. Remove the peppers from the pan and set them to cool in a dish large and deep enough to take the grilled fish fillets as well.

When the pepper rings are cool, place the fillets on top, skin side uppermost. While the fish is still warm, pour the chilli mixture over and leave them to marinate in the fridge for 2 hours. Remove the chilled fish from the chilli marinade and reserve the marinating liquid, which will be used as a dressing.

For the cod roe: Add 1 tbsp of oil to a sauté pan and lightly fry the slices of cod roe on both sides until they are a golden brown.

To serve, place one large or two small warm cod roe slices on each serving plate and position a cold gurnard fillet, with their browned skins showing, on top. Put some pepper rings on the plates, around the fillets, spoon over the chilli dressing, scatter the salted capers and basil leaves evenly between the plates, and garnish with some fresh fennel.

Pan-fried wood pigeon
on a bed of wild mushroom risotto

The combination of the earthy mushroom risotto, the succulent wood pigeon and the slight acidity of the vinaigrette make this dish a favourite of mine. Wood pigeon is an inexpensive bird that is full of flavour. However, it must be served pink – never overcook it or you'll end up with something resembling a piece of dry leather.

for the risotto

25g dried porcini (available from
　delicatessens and good
　supermarkets)
100ml hot water
25g unsalted butter
2 tbsp olive oil
1 small red onion, peeled and finely
　chopped
2 cloves of garlic, finely chopped
1 pinch of chilli powder
50g risotto rice (Arborio or Carnaroli)
570ml hot chicken stock (readymade is
　fine)
150g fresh wild mushrooms (any
　combination will do), roughly
　chopped
a squeeze of lemon juice
25g Parmesan cheese, grated

2 tbsp flat leaf parsley, chopped
Maldon sea salt and freshly ground
　black pepper

for the pan-fried wood pigeon

2 wood pigeon, with the breasts and
　legs removed
a little vegetable oil, for frying

for the vinaigrette

approximately 1 tbsp of the juices
　from the rested pigeon pieces
3 tbsp extra virgin olive oil
1 tbsp sherry vinegar
Maldon sea salt and freshly ground
　black pepper

for the garnish

some dressed mixed salad leaves

For the risotto: Firstly, soak the porcini for 30 minutes in the hot water, drain them and roughly chop them up, reserving the strained liquid. Then put half the butter, 1 tbsp of the olive oil and the chopped onion into a heavy-based pan and cook gently until the onion is soft and golden brown. Expect this to take about 3 minutes. Add half the garlic, the soaked porcini and the chilli and cook for another minute. Now add the rice and stir around for a minute until the rice is coated with the oil and butter. Next, mix the reserved porcini liquid with the chicken stock and add enough of this mixture to cover the rice. Allow it to simmer gently until the liquid is almost completely absorbed. Continue adding about a ladleful of the stock mixture at a time, allowing the rice to absorb most of it before adding more. Stir occasionally to prevent the rice sticking. The rice is cooked when there is still bite to it but it is not completely dry. This should take around 20 minutes but the only way to be sure is to taste the rice. While you are adding the stock mixture to the rice, sauté the wild mushrooms, in a separate pan, for 1–2 minutes before adding the rest of the garlic to the sauté pan. Continue sautéing for another 2–3 minutes until the mushrooms are cooked. Add the sautéed mushrooms, the lemon juice, the remaining butter, the Parmesan, the chopped parsley and the seasoning to the rice and mix well.

For the pan-fried wood pigeon: Preheat the oven to 170°C (gas mark 3). About 10 minutes before the rice is ready, cook off the pigeon breasts and legs in a frying pan with the oil over a medium heat for no longer than 2 minutes on each side. Remove them from the pan and put them in the oven on top of a small upturned plate that is sitting on top of a larger plate. This will allow the juices to run down on to the larger plate where they will be caught, and it will also prevent the meat lying in its own juices. Leave the meat to rest like this in the oven for 4–5 minutes. Remove the pigeon pieces from the oven and horizontally slice each of the breasts twice.

For the vinaigrette: Mix together the juices that have come from the rested pigeon pieces, the virgin olive oil and the sherry vinegar and season to taste.

To serve, place a neat pile of risotto in the centre of each of the 4 serving plates. Put 1 pigeon leg next to each mound of risotto and fan 3 slices of pigeon breast on top of the rice mounds. Put some mixed salad leaves around the plate and drizzle a little vinaigrette over the pigeon pieces and the salad leaves.

Lemon tart

with white rum

This lemon tart provides a wonderful end to a meal. With its full sharp lemon flavour – produced by using all of the lemons, not just the juice and zest – it has a real Mediterranean quality to it.

for the pastry	for the filling	for the garnish
100g unsalted butter, diced	4 medium-sized lemons	some crème fraîche,
200g plain flour	200g caster sugar	whipped double cream
100g icing sugar	3 whole large eggs	or a raspberry coulis
a pinch of salt	55ml white rum	
3–4 tbsp dry white wine, chilled	150g unsalted butter, softened and cut into small pieces	

For the pastry case: Rub the butter into the flour until the mixture resembles coarse breadcrumbs. Mix in the icing sugar and salt and then combine the mixture with the white wine to give a soft but rollable dough. Wrap the pastry in cling film and allow it to rest in the fridge for 1–2 hours.

Preheat the oven at 200°C (gas mark 6). Roll out the dough and use it to line a lightly buttered 23cm flan case. Prick the dough with a fork in several places, cover the base with greaseproof paper and fill the tart case with ceramic baking beans (dried beans or pasta shapes will work just as well). Bake blind for 10 minutes. Now take the tart case from the oven and remove the beans and greaseproof paper.

For the filling: Reduce the oven temperature to 150°C (gas mark 2). Slice the lemons and remove the seeds. Put the lemon slices in a food processor and chop to a pulp. Pour the puréed lemons into a mixing bowl and add the sugar, eggs, rum and softened butter. Beat well to combine using a hand beater or wooden spoon. Pour the lemon filling into the tart case and bake it for 40 minutes. The filling should be nicely browned when done so allow a few extra minutes if you think it needs it. Remove the tart from the oven and allow it to cool.

To serve, cut the cold tart into generous wedges, place one on each serving plate and present it with the crème fraîche, whipped double cream or perhaps even a homemade raspberry coulis as shown.

Dunain Park Hotel

near Inverness
EDWARD AND ANN NICOLL

Dunain Park is a very elegant house, set in the most lovely, tranquil gardens some two miles outside Inverness on the Loch Ness road. Inside, the house feels like a private home, except that it is a good deal more comfortable than most homes and rather more smartly decorated too. Dunain is a haven of peace and it has been the home and workplace of Edward and Ann Nicoll for the past seventeen years.

As with every establishment in this book, the food is the important lure to Dunain, but the comfort and attention to detail in every other aspect are bonuses. Ann is the inspiration in the kitchen. For the first seven years of their time here, she worked in a French restaurant for one week each year and she gives credit to Sonia Stevenson for inspiring her. Ann is assisted by her daughter Nicola, who created the delicious plum and port torte that follows, as well as Maree McDonough, who created the pan-fried cod and the wild boar dishes.

Everybody at Dunain agrees that it is essential to love food – and to love eating! They focus on seeking out the very best supplies, whether meat, fish, cheese, fruit or vegetables, although for some fruit and vegetables – courgettes, cabbages, spinach and several types of lettuce, fruits and berries – they don't have to look too far as these are grown in the Dunain gardens. The wine list at Dunain is equally impressive, with nearly all their wines coming from Lay and Wheeler, and you also have over two hundred single malt whiskies to choose from.

In the very best tradition of true Highland hospitality, excellent afternoon teas are served at Dunain Park and these prove to be a major attraction in themselves.

DUNAIN PARK HOTEL

Starter

Pan-fried cod
with banana salsa and a spiced coconut
and chilli cappuccino

Wine suggestion: Crozes-Hermitage Blanc,
2000, Domaine Pochon (France)

Main course

Wild boar
with beetroot risotto, Parmesan tuilles and
a bitter chocolate oil

Wine suggestion: Rioja Reserva, 1997, Bodegas
Murua, El Ciego (Spain)

Dessert

Plum and port torte

Wine suggestion: Chambers' Rutherglen
Muscadelle, Rosewood Vineyard, Victoria
(Australia)

Pan-fried cod

with banana salsa and a spiced coconut and chilli cappuccino

This little starter is just packed with flavours waiting to jump out at you. The meaty texture of the cod and the refreshing banana salsa go well together. And the contrast between the salsa and the cappuccino, with its punchy flavour, is interesting. If cod is unavailable, other fish, such as sea bass, mullet or snapper, will also work well.

for the spiced coconut and chilli
  cappuccino
1 stalk of lemon grass or a few sprigs
  of lemon balm
1 fresh red chilli, cut in half with the
  seeds and pith discarded
1 piece of fresh ginger (1cm x 1cm),
  peeled and roughly chopped
275ml double cream
55ml fish stock (readymade is fine)
55ml spiced rum
55ml Malibu
2 tins of coconut cream
salt and freshly ground black pepper
150ml semi-skimmed milk

for the cod
1 x 750g cod fillet, with the skin on
salt and freshly ground black pepper
a little olive oil and unsalted butter,
  for frying

for the banana salsa
2 good-sized ripe bananas
a bunch of fresh coriander

for the garnish
zest of 1 lemon, blanched
zest of 1 lime, blanched

For the spiced coconut and chilli cappuccino: If you are using lemon grass, cut the hard ends off it, remove the outer hard husks and crush well to extract the maximum flavour. Put all the ingredients, except the semi-skimmed milk, into a pan and place it over a very low heat. Allow the flavours to infuse but do not let it boil. After about half an hour, remove the pan from the heat, cover it and leave the sauce to cool. Now remove the chilli, lemon grass and ginger from the sauce, add the milk and check the seasoning. Using a whisk or hand blender, whisk the sauce until a cappuccino-like froth appears.

For the cod: If you have a whole fillet, cut it into 4 portions or you can ask your fishmonger to do this for you. Wash the fish well, pat it dry and put it in the fridge until needed. Season the cod portions, heat the olive oil in a non-stick frying pan, place the fish, skin sides down, in the hot oil and cook the portions for about 1 minute or until they are golden in colour. Add a little butter, turn the cod portions over and cook them for a further few minutes on both sides. If your fish is quite thick, place it in an ovenproof dish and put it in a hot oven for a few minutes to cook through.

For the banana salsa: Roughly chop the bananas and coriander and thoroughly mix them together.

To serve, put a 6cm cutter or mould in the centre of a serving plate, spoon some banana salsa into it, remove the cutter or mould – it is only there to give the salsa shape – and repeat for the other 3 plates. Place a cod portion on top of the banana salsa and drizzle the cappuccino sauce around the plate. Garnish with the blanched zest of lemon and lime.

Wild boar

with beetroot risotto, Parmesan tuilles and a bitter
chocolate oil

Here at Dunain Park, it is our philosophy to use only the finest and freshest
produce available. In keeping with this, we have sourced wild boar as an
alternative to pork. We have a local supplier and together we have seen the
popularity of wild boar steadily increase. I feel it is a healthier choice compared to
pork from mass-reared pigs and the meat is extremely tender. Its distinctive gamey
taste is not as strong as venison and this gives it wider appeal.

for the beetroot risotto
50g butter
1 tbsp olive oil
1 red onion, finely chopped
1 or 2 sprigs of fresh thyme
275g beetroot, cooked and chopped
350g Arborio rice
1.5 litre chicken stock
1 tsp salt
a splash of red wine
30ml raspberry vinegar or red wine
    vinegar

for the chocolate oil
100g bitter chocolate
4 heaped tsp cocoa powder
30ml quality olive oil
100ml hazelnut-infused oil

for the wild boar
1kg tenderloin or fillet of wild boar
45ml olive oil
sea salt and freshly ground black
    pepper

for the Parmesan tuilles
100g Parmesan cheese, finely grated

For the beetroot risotto: Melt half the butter in a large deep frying pan, add the
olive oil, cook the onion on a gentle heat for about 10 minutes and then add the
thyme. Now add 100g of the beetroot and cook for another 2–3 minutes. Add the
rice and cook gently for 5–6 minutes, stirring continuously. Add a ladleful of stock,
plus 1 tsp salt, and continue to cook slowly, stirring all the time, until the liquid is
absorbed. Keep adding a ladleful of stock at a time until the rice is swollen and
just cooked. Expect this to take roughly 15 minutes. Now add the wine, the
vinegar and the rest of the beetroot. Check the seasoning, remove the pan from
the heat and beat in the remaining butter.

For the Parmesan tuilles: Preheat the oven to 200°C (gas mark 6). Press the finely grated cheese together to make 4 discs about 3–4mm thick. Place them on an Exopat baking mat or on a baking sheet lined with non-stick baking parchment and bake them in the oven for approximately 6–7 minutes. Remove the tuilles from the oven and leave them on the mat or baking tray to cool and crisp up.

For the chocolate oil: Combine all of the ingredients in a large bowl and place it over a pan of hot, not boiling, water. Allow the chocolate to melt, stirring occasionally. Store in a warm place until serving.

For the wild boar: Preheat the oven to 200°C (gas mark 6). Trim off any sinews and divide the meat into four pieces. Put a light covering of olive oil into a hot pan and seal the meat on both sides. Transfer the meat to an oven tray, season it well and roast it in the oven for about 8–10 minutes.

To serve, place a 6cm cutter or mould in the centre of a serving plate. Put a layer of beetroot risotto in it, place a Parmesan tuille on top of the rice and then add another layer of risotto. Now remove the cutter or mould and repeat for the other 3 plates. Slice the meat and either arrange it on the plate next to the risotto or on top of it as shown. Stir the chocolate oil well and drizzle it round the plate.

Plum and port torte

A walled garden at Dunain Park yields an abundance of plums in the late summer and they are perfect for this light fresh summer torte. Allow at least $2^1/_2$ hours – this includes time to chill the pastry – for preparing and cooking this dish.

for the pastry
175g plain flour
1 level dsp caster sugar
a pinch of ground ginger (optional)
100g salted butter, softened
$1–1^1/_2$ tbsp cold water

60ml runny honey
1 level tsp ground cinnamon
grated rind of 1 orange
1 pinch of grated nutmeg
1 heaped tbsp of agar-agar powder or
    agar-agar flakes (gelatin is also fine)

for the filling
700g ripe plums
60ml ruby port

for the garnish
a little icing sugar, for dusting
some lightly whipped double cream

For the pastry: Mix all the dry ingredients together and rub the softened butter into them until the mixture resembles coarse breadcrumbs. Gradually add the water until the dough is just moist enough to hold together. Lightly flour your hands and form the pastry dough into a round, pressing the dough down and wrapping it in cling film. Chill the pastry dough in the fridge for half an hour. Roll the pastry out and use it to line a 23cm lightly greased loose-bottom flan ring that is at least 4cm deep. Trim the edges and reserve the trimmed pastry for later. Cover the pastry base with greaseproof paper and fill the flan ring with ceramic baking beans (dried beans or pasta shapes will work just as well). The beans will stop the base rising and prevent the sides from collapsing during what is called 'blind baking'. Put the prepared flan ring into the fridge to rest for at least 1 hour (overnight if possible). Preheat the oven to 190°C (gas mark 5). Bake the pastry case blind for 10 minutes, remove the beans or pasta and greaseproof paper and then return the pastry case to the oven for a further 5 minutes.

For the filling: Keep the oven at 190°C (gas mark 5). Put everything, except the agar-agar, into a pan and cook for 10 minutes, until the fruit is soft. An aroma reminiscent of mulled wine will be released. Now set the cooked plums aside to cool. When cool, sprinkle in the agar-agar and return the pan to a medium heat for 3–5 minutes, stirring occasionally. Pour the filling into the pastry case and decorate with strips of the remaining pastry to form a lattice pattern or just leave it plain if you prefer. Cook the torte in the oven for 25–30 minutes.

To serve, cut the warm or chilled torte into generous wedges. Place a wedge of torte on each of the 4 serving plates, dust them with the icing sugar and present with some lightly whipped cream.

Peat turfs, Isle of Harris

Kinloch Lodge

Sleat, Isle of Skye

GODFREY AND CLAIRE MACDONALD

Godfrey and I are in our thirtieth year of running our home, Kinloch, as a hotel. Neither of us have had any formal training in hotel management or catering. We knew at the start what we wanted to give our guests, which is just what we would expect to find in as remote and beautiful a place as Kinloch, set at the foot of a mountain and directly above a sea loch. Along with the external peace and tranquillity must go log fires and comfortable drawing rooms to sit and snooze in and a mass of books to browse through.

We have three drawing rooms between the two houses that comprise Kinloch; the Lodge and Kinloch itself. The Lodge is a very old hunting lodge, thus some of the bedrooms are small, but to us it is imperative that both the beds and pillows are of the utmost comfort, so we change them every three to four years. The bedrooms all have televisions, hair dryers, trouser presses, well-placed electrical sockets and well-equipped bathrooms – everything a guest would expect to find in a hotel these days.

Our food is not chef cooking. We are a team of cooks, and our desire is to produce food which is a treat to eat, but we bow to no current culinary fashion. We use the best produce in the world, which is fish and shellfish on our doorstep, and meat from Duncan Fraser, surely the best butcher in the UK, who hangs his Scottish raised meat (beef, lamb, pork and venison) for a sufficient length of time to ensure the tenderness and flavour essential for us and our guests. So many of the vegetables we use, all the salad leaves, herbs and much of the soft fruit, are grown locally here in Skye. The wild mushrooms that we don't pick ourselves locally are cultivated on the mainland, near Kyle of Lochalsh.

We make everything ourselves, from the breakfast scones and marmalade to the fudge we serve with coffee after dinner. Our breakfasts are as important to us in their quality and content as our dinners, but I suppose our puddings could be considered our speciality, probably inspired by my own sweet tooth. We aim to cook food in its natural season to Scotland and Skye, so food plays as vital a role in the day-to-day running of Kinloch as the warmth, welcome and general comfort.

Claire Macdonald, Proprietor and Cook

KINLOCH LODGE

Starter

Smoked haddock quenelles
with chive cream sauce

Wine suggestion: St Francis Chardonnay Estate
Reserve, 1999, Sonoma County (USA)

Main course

Pork fillets with prune and sage stuffing
served with a prune, shallot
and sage cream sauce

Wine suggestion: Hochar Père et Fils, 1998,
Château Musar (Lebanon)

Dessert

Lemon curd parfait
with berries

Wine suggestion: Pacherenc du Vic-Bilh, 1999,
Saint Albert (France)

Menu

Smoked haddock quenelles
with chive cream sauce

Traditionally, quenelles are made using pike – a fish that I find rather uninteresting. However, quenelles can be made with any type of fish and this smoked haddock version is my favourite.

for the quenelles
450g filleted undyed
  smoked haddock, cut
  into chunks and all
  bones removed
1 large egg
2 egg whites
300ml double cream

10g fresh parsley,
  preferably flat-leaf
a good grinding of black
  pepper
a grating of nutmeg
500–750ml vegetable
  stock

for the sauce
300ml double cream
15ml lemon juice
2 tbsp fresh chives,
  snipped

For the quenelles: Put the fish chunks into a food processor and whizz to break the fish up before adding the egg, egg whites, cream and parsley. Continue whizzing until everything is well combined and then season the mixture with the pepper and nutmeg. Scrape the mixture into a bowl, cover it with cling film and leave it in the fridge for several hours. If it is more convenient, making this a day in advance is fine. Pour the vegetable stock into a wide saucepan – I use a large sauté pan – to a depth of 6–8cm and bring it to the boil. Using two tablespoons, form the fish mixture into egg shapes, as tidily as possible, and, when the stock is fast boiling, slip the quenelles into the pan. Poach them for 5 minutes, turning each over once during the cooking time. When they are cooked, carefully remove them from the stock, using a slotted spoon, and place them in a warm heatproof dish.

For the sauce: Make the simple cream sauce by simmering the double cream with the lemon juice for 4–5 minutes. The cream will thicken and become a deep ivory colour. Just before serving, stir in the snipped chives but beware of adding the chives too soon prior to serving because, if they are left in the sauce for too long, they will turn greyish in colour and lose their fresh taste.

    To serve, pour the sauce over the warm quenelles in the dish or, if you are serving them individually, spoon some of the sauce over each serving.

Pork fillets with prune and sage stuffing

served with a prune, shallot and sage cream sauce

This is a delicious moist stuffing and the flavours complement the pork so well. It makes an elegant main course that is simple and convenient to prepare.

for the prune and sage stuffing
45ml extra virgin olive oil
2 sticks of celery, trimmed of stringy
  bits and thinly sliced
3 banana shallots or 6 smaller ones,
  peeled and very finely diced
50g fresh white breadcrumbs
1 tbsp fresh sage leaves, chopped
4 no-soak prunes, chopped small (if
  you dip the knife into very hot
  water, it will prevent the prunes
  sticking as you chop)
$^1/_2$ tsp salt and a good grinding of
  black pepper

for the shallot and sage cream sauce
300ml red wine
3 banana shallots or 6 smaller ones,
  peeled and very finely diced
300ml double cream
3 fresh sage leaves, chopped
4 no-soak prunes, chopped small (see
  stuffing recipe for ease of chopping)
$^1/_2$ tsp salt and a good grinding of
  black pepper

for the accompaniments
boiled new potatoes
a green vegetable of your choice

for the pork fillets
2 whole pork fillets
50g unsalted butter, melted

For the prune and sage stuffing: Make the stuffing first. Heat the olive oil in a saucepan and sauté the sliced celery and finely diced shallots over a low–medium heat, for around 10–15 minutes, until very soft. Put the breadcrumbs into a bowl and add the sautéed celery and shallots, together with the prunes, sage leaves, salt and pepper. Mix everything together very thoroughly.

For the pork fillets: Preheat the oven to 200°C (gas mark 6). Prepare the pork fillets by laying them on a board and trimming off any membranous tissue. Slit each fillet in half lengthways, taking care not to cut right through them. Spread out the fillets, cover them with cling film and bash them flatter with a rolling pin until they are about 1cm thick. Divide the stuffing into 2 equal amounts and put it down the centre of each flattened fillet. Roll the meat over the stuffing and put the stuffed fillets on to a baking tray or roasting tin. Brush each fillet very well with the melted butter and roast them in the oven for 25 minutes. Brush them with more melted butter once or twice during their roasting time.

For the shallot and sage cream sauce: Put the red wine and finely diced shallots into a saucepan and simmer until the wine has almost entirely disappeared. As the wine reduces the shallots will soften. Stir in the cream, sage leaves and prunes, season with salt and pepper and simmer for a further 3–4 minutes.

To serve, cut the stuffed pork fillets into thick slices, arrange them on the 4 serving plates and spoon the sauce over them. Serve the sliced pork with boiled new potatoes and a green vegetable of your choice.

Lemon curd parfait
with berries

When served on top of summer berries, this is one of the best puds imaginable.
Any berries that are in season are suitable or try a mixture of, for example,
raspberries and blackcurrants, or blueberries and brambles. However, the parfait is
also delicious throughout the year simply served alone, piled into glasses.

for the lemon curd
110g butter, cut into
  chunks
110g granulated or
  caster sugar
2 large egg yolks and 2
  large eggs, well beaten
  together

zest and juice of 2
  lemons, well washed

for the parfait
2 large egg whites
50g icing sugar, sieved
300ml double cream,
  whipped, not too stiffly

for the berries
350g seasonal berries,
  such as blueberries or
  blackcurrants

For the lemon curd: Put all the ingredients into a Pyrex or similar heatproof bowl
sitting over a saucepan of simmering water. Stir until the butter has melted and
the sugar has dissolved. Continue heating, giving an occasional stir until the curd
is thick. Take the bowl off the heat and allow the curd to cool. This quantity will
give you more than you need for this dish but that is no hardship as it keeps well
in the fridge and is delicious spread on warm toast or scones.

For the parfait: Using scrupulously clean whisks, whisk the egg whites until they are
fairly stiff. While still whisking, gradually add the sieved icing sugar, a spoonful at a
time, until it is all incorporated. With a metal spoon, fold the meringue-like mixture,
together with 4 generous tablespoons of the lemon curd, into the whipped cream.

For the berries: Gently heat the berries just until their juices run. There is no need
to sweeten blueberries but, if you use blackcurrants, add sugar or honey to taste.
Allow the berries to cool.

   To serve, divide the berries between 4 large glasses or glass goblets and spoon
the lemon curd parfait on top. I think any garnish is superfluous here – the
contrast in colour between the berries and the parfait is good enough. However,
to create an even more stunning effect, you could cut lemons into thin slices and
arrange them around the inside of the glasses.

Loch Ewe, Wester Ross

Kylesku Hotel
Kylesku
PATRICK AND IMELDA GILMOUR

Immortalised in song, the waters of Kylesku, surrounded by the rugged mountains of Sutherland, are simply beautiful and so dramatic that it is easy to understand the inspiration of the songwriter.

Kylesku Hotel is a small white building that dates back to 1883. It is situated right above the slipway from where the ferry crossed the waters until the bridge was built around the corner and upstream in 1984. In such unspoilt terrain, the wildlife – deer, badgers, pine martens, wild cats, otters and seals, not to mention a huge variety of birds – makes Kylesku a perfect haven to stay at. Also on offer is some of the best walking and climbing imaginable. But the other great reason for visiting Kylesku is the warmth of welcome from Patrick and Imelda Gilmour, who have owned and run the hotel for nearly three years.

The hotel has a picturesque dining room with breathtaking views across the waters to the mountains beyond, where the light changes every minute to create a captivating backdrop for the delicious food being served there – and the presentation and sheer taste of everything we ate were a testament to the quality of produce and preparation. The menu is largely fish and shellfish, most of which is landed on the slipway beside the hotel, but other fish comes from nearby Lochinver. The cheeses come from the Achiltibuie Smokehouse. In the kitchen are Daniel McGalpine from South Africa, and his second chef, David Paine, from Lairg. There is a separate menu for the public bar and it offers equally enticing dishes. Each one is made to order and it is no wonder that, on busy days in the summer months, they can serve up to two hundred meals a day.

Kylesku Hotel combines everything I consider to be essential for a visitor to the Highlands – comfort, really good food in an old hotel with all the present-day amenities, and truly spectacular scenery wherever you look.

KYLESKU HOTEL

Starter

Venison terrine
with onion and beetroot chutney

Wine suggestion: Cabernet Sauvignon,
2000 (South Africa)

Main course

Grilled langoustines
with garlic mayonnaise

Wine suggestion: Maçon Lugny Les Charmes
A.C., 1999/2000 (France)

Dessert

Bread-and-butter pudding
with a warm ginger cream sauce

Wine suggestion: A late harvest orange Muscat
or Flora, 2000/2001 (Australia)

Venison terrine

with onion and beetroot chutney

The venison needs to be marinated for at least 12 hours so you will need to start this dish the day before serving. You could make the chutney the day before too.

for the marinade
200ml red wine
55ml olive oil
4 cloves of garlic, chopped

for the onion and beetroot chutney
25g butter
2 medium onions, finely sliced
1 beetroot, grated
1 tbsp tomato purée
2 cloves
2 fresh bay leaves
1 tbsp granulated sugar
2 tbsp white wine vinegar

for the venison terrine
700g venison, diced

1 large egg, lightly beaten
1 tbsp soft green peppercorns
salt and freshly ground black pepper
1 clove of garlic, crushed
1 tsp dried mixed herbs
1 onion, finely diced
1 carrot, finely diced
1 red pepper, finely diced
1 chicken breast
6 rashers of unsmoked back bacon

for the accompaniments
a selection of dressed mixed salad
    leaves
red, green and yellow peppers, thinly
    sliced and blanched
4 portions of hot toast

For the marinade: Mix all of the marinade ingredients together in a large bowl, add the diced venison and marinate it in the fridge for a minimum of 12 hours.

For the onion and beetroot chutney: Melt the butter and sweat the finely sliced onions over a very low heat for around 10 minutes, until they become soft and transparent. Add the rest of the ingredients and continue cooking over a low heat for about half an hour, stirring occasionally, until the mixture has reduced and thickened.

For the venison terrine: Preheat the oven to 190°C (gas mark 5). Remove the diced venison from the marinade and pass the meat through a mincer fitted with a coarse mincing plate. Add the beaten egg, soft green peppercorns, salt, pepper, crushed garlic and mixed herbs and combine. Next add the finely diced onion, carrot and red pepper and thoroughly mix everything together. Trim the chicken breast and cut it into finger-sized pieces. Line a 900g terrine with the bacon, allowing the rashers to hang down over the edge. Half-fill the terrine with the venison mixture and make a groove down the middle of it using the back of a spoon. Put the chicken breast pieces into the groove and then fill the terrine with the remaining venison mixture. Press the mixture down firmly and flip the overhanging bacon rashers over the top of it. Cover the terrine with its lid or, if it does not have a lid, use tinfoil. Place the terrine in a bain-marie (an oven tray filled with enough water to come halfway up the terrine) and cook it in the oven for $1^1/_2$ hours. Leave the terrine in its container to cool, then remove it from the terrine and cut it into thick slices.

To serve, put a small bed of mixed dressed salad leaves in the centre of each of the 4 serving plates and place a slice of terrine on top of them with a garnish of the blanched peppers. Spoon some onion and beetroot chutney on to the side of the plates and present the dish with the hot toast.

Grilled langoustines
with garlic mayonnaise

Here at Kylesku, we are so lucky because our shellfish is caught almost literally on our doorstep, ensuring it is as fresh as can be. When you are fortunate enough to have such fresh produce, it is often best to do as little as possible to it – as this extremely simple dish proves.

for the garlic mayonnaise	for the langoustines	for the accompaniments
1 egg	28 live langoustines	some mixed dressed salad leaves
2 tsp white wine vinegar	a little garlic oil	4 portions of freshly fried chips
$^1/_2$ tsp salt	a small glass of dry white wine	
300ml olive oil	freshly ground black pepper	
3 cloves of garlic, finely chopped		

For the garlic mayonnaise: Put the egg, vinegar and salt into a food processor, turn it on and slowly add the oil through the hole in the lid. Add the chopped garlic and put the mayonnaise into an airtight container in the fridge until required.

For the langoustines: Put the live langoustines into a pan of cold water and bring them to the boil. As soon as the water is boiling, take the pan off the heat and cool by running cold water into it. Once they are cold, put 7 langoustines on each of four skewers, sprinkle them with the garlic oil and place them under a hot grill for about 7 minutes, turning them several times. Remove the langoustines from the grill and splash the white wine over them.

To serve, put a bed of mixed salad leaves in the centre of each of the 4 serving plates and place the langoustine skewers on top. Put a generous spoonful of garlic mayonnaise on the side of each plate and present the langoustines with the chips.

Bread-and-butter pudding
with a warm ginger cream sauce

Bread-and-butter pudding may not sound like the most glamorous of desserts but it is one of our best-sellers. The warm ginger cream sauce perfectly offsets the milkiness of the pudding.

for the bread-and-butter pudding	for the warm ginger cream sauce
275ml milk	275ml double cream
50g caster sugar	10g fresh root ginger, peeled and
2 large eggs	grated
12 slices of white bread	1 tsp caster sugar
10g butter	
10g sultanas	
10g demerara sugar	

For the bread-and-butter pudding: Preheat the oven to 180°C (gas mark 4). Pour the milk into a saucepan and add the caster sugar. Leave the pan on a gentle heat until the milk is warm and the sugar has dissolved. Meanwhile, break the eggs into a bowl and lightly beat them. Add the warm milk to the beaten eggs, whisking all the time. Strain the mixture through a sieve. Butter 4 ramekins. Cut the bread into 12 discs of the same size as your ramekins and butter the bread discs on both sides. Sprinkle some sultanas and demerara sugar over the bottom of the ramekins and place three discs of bread on top of each. Pour the milk, sugar and egg mixture over the bread discs and leave them for 20 minutes, until the bread has absorbed the liquid. Now top up the ramekins with any remaining liquid. Fill a high-sided oven tray with enough water to come three-quarters of the way up the ramekins. Put the ramekins in the oven tray and bake them for 20 minutes.

For the warm ginger cream sauce: Pour the cream into a saucepan and warm it through, taking care not to let it to boil. Remove the pan from the heat, add the grated ginger and caster sugar and allow the ginger to infuse for 20 minutes over a low heat. Strain the sauce to remove the grated ginger.

To serve, slide a knife round the edge of the ramekins to loosen the puddings and then turn them out on to the middle of the 4 serving plates. Pour the warm ginger cream sauce around the outside of each pudding.

Near Broadford, Isle of Skye

Leachin House
by Tarbert, Harris
DIARMUID AND LINDA WOOD

For eleven years, Diarmuid and Linda Wood have lived in Leachin House, overlooking the dreamy West Loch one mile from Tarbert. From the outside, it looks a solid, comforting house and, as soon as you enter, you are enveloped in its atmosphere of welcome. You are also immediately aware of being in a very well-decorated home. Leachin is comfortable and filled with objects of fascination. In the drawing room, in the three bedrooms – which are each so individually pretty and contain everything a guest could want for warmth and comfort – and in the dining room – where the guests eat communally, overlooking the loch – everything is immaculate, yet completely lacking in the formality this might imply. The dining room is a most intriguing room, decorated in lovely hand-painted French wallpaper with original, intricate gold leaf in the design. Because of the benign climate of the Outer Hebrides, this treasure is extremely well preserved. On the wall is an old photograph dating from the late nineteenth century of the original owners of the house and the same wallpaper is clearly visible behind them.

Linda teaches French locally but she still has time to do all the cooking for her guests. She is a self-taught cook who simply loves food and she is very particular about the produce she buys. She uses as much locally sourced food as she can get and is especially grateful for the peat-smoked salmon from North Uist and, of course, for Salar's flaky hot-smoked salmon, also from North Uist. The Gourmet's Lair, in Inverness, is her great source of delicatessen foods, and they will helpfully send her items by post, too, in between her visits to the city.

Diarmuid is an invaluable host who delights in advising his guests, during their days on Harris and Lewis, on walks and visits to local places of interest – often pointing them in the direction of places that are left out of even the best guide books. He can also suggest itineraries to suit the weather on any particular day. Such local knowledge and his enthusiasm for the wildlife, walks and heritage are too rarely found in our trade and this, combined with Linda's fantastic cooking skills, makes Leachin a gem of a guest house.

Linda Wood, Proprietor and Cook

LEACHIN HOUSE

Starter

Tomato and smoked cheese tartlets
with asparagus and dressed salad leaves

Wine suggestion: a good quality French
Chardonnay or Italian Verdicchio

Main course

Fillets of salmon
with a horseradish crust and chive sauce

Wine suggestion: a good quality French
Chardonnay or Italian Verdicchio

Dessert

Raspberry and hazelnut roulade with
raspberry coulis

Wine suggestion: a good quality French
Chardonnay or Italian Verdicchio

Menu

Tomato and smoked cheese tartlets

with asparagus and dressed salad leaves

The Mediterranean flavour of this dish is nicely enhanced by the smokiness of the Scottish cheddar. The Orkney, Arran and Summer Isles varieties of smoked cheddar work particularly well.

for the tartlets
350g puff pastry
  (readymade is fine)
20–25ml pesto sauce
  (readymade is fine)
75g smoked cheddar,
  grated
3 tomatoes, sliced
4 fresh basil leaves,
  chopped
20ml olive oil

salt and freshly ground
  black pepper

for the asparagus
16 asparagus spears,
  peeled and trimmed

for the dressed salad
  leaves
30ml olive oil
45ml corn oil

30ml red wine vinegar
6ml French mustard
1 tsp caster sugar
1 clove of garlic,
  crushed
salt and freshly ground
  black pepper
a selection of colourful
  mixed salad leaves

For the tartlets: Preheat the oven to 200°C (gas mark 6). Roll the pastry out to a thickness of 3mm and cut out four discs of a diameter of 15cm. Line four 10cm tartlet tins with the pastry discs, pressing them well down and trimming off any excess around the rims. Prick the pastry all over with a fork. Spread a heaped teaspoon of pesto sauce over the bases, put a heaped tablespoon of grated cheese on top and press down firmly. Next top with 3 overlapping slices of tomato, followed by some chopped basil. Drizzle a teaspoon of olive oil over the filling of each tartlet and then season them with salt and black pepper. Bake the tartlets in the oven for 20–25 minutes until they are golden brown.

For the asparagus: Steam the asparagus for no more than 4–5 minutes.

For the dressing: Put all the ingredients except the salad leaves into a screw-top jar and shake well until they are all incorporated. When you are ready to serve the tartlets, give the jar a good shake and dress the leaves.

To serve, put the dressed leaves on one side of the serving plates, and place 4 asparagus spears and a warm tartlet next to them.

Fillets of salmon

with a horseradish crust and chive sauce

If you are a bit wary about making hollandaise sauce, try this chive sauce instead. It is much easier and just as good.

for the chive sauce
275ml double cream
2 tsp Dijon mustard
2 tsp English mustard (readymade)
2 tsp creamed horseradish
2 tsp freshly squeezed lemon juice
2 tbsp fresh chives, snipped

for the horseradish crust
2 tbsp creamed horseradish
1 egg yolk
50g coarse fresh white breadcrumbs
2 tbsp fresh parsley, chopped

for the salmon
4 x 175g salmon fillets, skinless and
   with all bones removed using
   tweezers
salt and freshly ground black pepper
a little flour, for dredging
1 tbsp vegetable oil
1 tbsp salted butter

for the accompaniments
boiled new potatoes
fresh green beans

For the chive sauce: Boil the double cream in a pan for 2 minutes until it has reduced and thickened slightly. Remove from the heat and whisk in the two mustards, the horseradish and the lemon juice. Cover the sauce and set it aside until you are ready to serve.

For the horseradish crust: Mix the horseradish and egg yolk together and pour the mixture on to one flat plate. On another flat plate, mix the breadcrumbs and parsley together.

For the salmon fillets: Preheat the oven to 180° (gas mark 4). Season each fillet with the salt and black pepper and then dredge the rounded upper sides with flour. Now dip the floured sides of each fillet in the horseradish and egg mixture, ensuring they are well coated. Next dip the coated side of the fillets into the breadcrumb mixture, pressing down firmly so that the fillets have a good covering of the crust mixture on them. Heat the oil in a heavy-based frying pan until very hot. Add the butter and then the fillets, crust side down. Cook for about 3 minutes until the breadcrumbs are nicely crisp and beginning to turn brown. Remove the salmon fillets from the pan and place them in an ovenproof dish, crust side up. Bake the crusted fillets for 5 minutes or until they are cooked through.

To serve, add the snipped chives to the sauce and warm it up, taking great care not to allow it to boil. Place a salmon fillet on each of the 4 pre-warmed plates and surround with the chive sauce. Present the dish with the boiled new potatoes and green beans.

Raspberry and hazelnut roulade

with raspberry coulis

This is particularly delicious when made using our locally grown raspberries.
However, these are only available for a short season here on Lewis and Harris and,
during the rest of the year, fresh supermarket ones or even frozen ones will work
almost as well.

for the meringue	for the raspberry coulis	for the roulade filling
100g hazelnuts, chopped (packet ones are ideal)	110g caster sugar	275ml double cream, whipped
1 tsp cornflour	150ml water	
1 tsp vanilla extract	225g raspberries (fresh if possible)	350g raspberries (fresh if possible)
1 tsp white wine vinegar	a little freshly squeezed lemon juice	
4 egg whites		a little sieved icing sugar, to serve
150g caster sugar		

For the meringue: Preheat the oven to 170°C (gas mark 3). Take a shallow baking
tin, measuring about 23cm x 33cm, and line it with baking parchment, snipping off
the corners so that it fits snugly. Dry-fry the chopped hazelnuts for 3–4 minutes
until they are light golden in colour. Cool the fried hazelnuts and then whiz them
to a powder in a food processor. In a small bowl, blend the cornflour, vanilla
extract and vinegar together to form a smooth paste. In a clean dry bowl, whisk the
egg whites until they stand in stiff peaks. Now gradually whisk in the sugar and the
cornflour paste, adding only a little of each at a time and ensuring that both are
well incorporated before adding any more. Once all the sugar and the cornflour
paste have been whisked into the egg whites, the mixture should be very white and
have a lovely rich texture. Reserve 2 tablespoons of the powdered hazelnuts and
then gently fold in the rest into the meringue mixture, using a metal spoon. Now
pour the mixture into the prepared baking tin, sprinkle over the reserved powdered
hazelnuts and bake the meringue in the oven for about 25 minutes. Remove the
meringue from the oven and allow it to cool in the baking tin.

For the raspberry coulis: Mix the sugar and water together in a pan, bring the
mixture to the boil and simmer it for a few minutes, ensuring all the sugar has
dissolved. Allow the sugar liquid to cool. Put the raspberries in a liquidiser and add
about two-thirds of the sugar liquid. Liquidise the mixture and then sieve it. Now

taste the raspberry coulis and adjust the sweetness if necessary, adding some lemon juice if you think it is too sweet or some more of the sugar liquid if it is not sweet enough.

For the roulade filling: When the meringue is cool, spread the whipped cream to within about 1cm of the edges. Scatter the raspberries all over and roll up the roulade, going from one short end to the other. Use the baking parchment to help with this. If the meringue cracks slightly, don't worry. Put the roulade on to a plate, dust it with the sieved icing sugar and cut it into thick slices.

To serve, put a pool of the raspberry coulis on each of the 4 serving plates and place a slice of roulade on top.

Near Holm Sound, Orkney

Near Tongue, Sutherland

Loch Bay Seafood Restaurant

Waternish, Isle of Skye

DAVID AND ALISON WILKINSON

A long white building on the loch front, Loch Bay Seafood Restaurant has an enticing, homely atmosphere, with warmth from a wood-burning stove greeting guests on arrival. David and Alison Wilkinson have spent their entire working lives in the catering business – they met when they were both working in a five-star hotel in Hampshire before David became a Michelin inspector. In 1981 they moved from London to the Highlands to convert and help run the prestigious Arisaig House, where they cooked and managed for seventeen years. From October 2002 it will cease to be a hotel, and Alison's parents will live in it as a private house.

David and Alison have owned and run Loch Bay for two years. David cooks in the restaurant while Alison looks after the guests. She is such a warm and welcoming person and sets the scene for a very happy meal, whether lunch or dinner. The restaurant interior is wood throughout, with a terracotta-tiled floor. The walls and shelves are filled with intriguing prints and objects, most notably a charming row of ducks above the wood stove.

The food at Loch Bay is simply the best fish and shellfish. This is the freshest produce imaginable, which is just what one would expect from both the restaurant's name and location. With the exception of the mussels, which they buy from Ian Mackinnon in Arisaig, all the shellfish is Skye-caught. The oysters are from Talisker, the scallops from Sconser and prawns from Willie Murdo's boat in Dunvegan. The rest of the fish used comes from Andy Race in Mallaig, Ian Clark in Buckie and Isle of Skye Seafoods in Broadford.

Both fish and shellfish are perfectly and simply cooked – brushed with olive oil and, in some cases, garlic and parsley butter. The mussels are steamed with onions and white wine. The puddings on the menu are as tantalising and delicious as the fish served before them – with the butteriest chocolate bread-and-butter pudding, a fine crème brûlée, a good cloutie dumpling and a most delectable vanilla ice cream with meringue and warm butterscotch sauce. The wine list is also very good – David buys his wines from David Bryant of Ardmore Wines and also from Justerini and Brooks.

LOCH BAY
SEAFOOD RESTAURANT

Starter

Seared squid

Wine suggestion: Muscadet Côtes de Grandlieu
Sur Lie, 1999 (France)

Main course

Grilled whole sea bass
brushed with a citrus emulsion

Wine suggestion: Best's Victoria Colombard,
1998 (Australia)

Dessert

Rhubarb fool

Wine suggestion: Muscat de Rivesaltes, 1999,
Château Cap de Fouste (France)

Menu

Seared squid

A recent TV programme on the Falkland Islands stated that most of the world's squid came from the South Atlantic waters. However we get ours from the Minch, the waters between the mainland West Coast of Scotland and the Western Isles. A good fishmonger will be able to offer squid ready prepared, with the nib, membrane, beak and ink sack removed. Ensure you get the small tentacles to add to the final dish. Allow at least 3 hours for the squid to marinate.

for the squid	4 cloves of garlic,	for the garnish
350–450g squid,	crushed	a selection of mixed
prepared by your	1 tbsp mixed fresh herbs	salad leaves
fishmonger	(parsley, dill, coriander	1 lemon, cut into
	and chives), chopped	wedges
for the marinade	salt and freshly ground	fresh dill, chives and
275ml good olive oil	black pepper	parsley, chopped

For the squid: Begin by blanching the squid, including the tentacles, in boiling salted water for 5 minutes and then refresh it in cold water. Now cut across the body of the squid at about 6mm intervals to produce slender rings of flesh.

For the marinade: Mix together all the ingredients and add the squid rings and tentacles, ensuring that the pieces are well covered. The squid needs to be marinated for at least 3 hours at room temperature before cooking. (You can store the marinated squid in a glass jar for up to two weeks, providing it is refrigerated and covered with oil. You will find that the oil will thicken and go cloudy. When you come to cook the stored squid, ensure most of the oil around it is shaken off.)

Take a heavy frying pan and preheat it for 3–4 minutes until it is moderately hot. Add the squid (no extra oil is necessary and take care not to put the garlic into the pan – it is only there to flavour the marinade). Cover the pan as the squid will spit badly and, keeping the temperature moderately hot, cook for 2 minutes, stirring once with a spatula and cooking for a further 2 minutes.

To serve, place a bed of salad leaves in the centre of each plate, place the cooked squid on top, a lemon wedge on the side and garnish with the fresh herbs.

Grilled whole sea bass
brushed with a citrus emulsion

The joy of serving sea bass cooked whole on the bone is that it ensures that it is moist and full of flavour. Get your fishmonger to prepare the fish by de-scaling them, removing the fins and heads and gutting them.

for the citrus emulsion
juice of ½ a large orange
juice of ½ a lemon
200ml olive oil
salt and black pepper

for the accompaniments
a little coarse sea salt
1 lemon, cut into wedges
boiled new potatoes
a green vegetable of your choice

for the fish
4 x 450g whole sea bass

For the emulsion: Put all the ingredients into a bowl and blend them together to form an emulsion.

For the fish: Preheat the grill for several minutes until it becomes really hot. Using a sharp knife, score the skin of the fish, to a depth of about 3mm, in 4 or 5 places on each side. Liberally brush each fish with the emulsion on both sides. Place the fish on a flat baking sheet and put them under the grill. Cook the sea bass for approximately 4 minutes on each side – the cooking time will vary according to the intensity of your grill. The oil in the emulsion should prevent the fish from sticking to the baking sheet. The fish is cooked when it is firm to the touch and the skin is beginning to turn brown and be crisp.

To serve, place a sea bass on each of the 4 serving plates and sprinkle some coarse sea salt over them. Present the fish with the new potatoes and green vegetables, with a lemon wedge on the side.

Rhubarb fool

The garden at Loch Bay is blessed with an abundance of delicately flavoured rhubarb. The young stalks are particularly suitable for this dessert.

for the rhubarb
900g young rhubarb
225g granulated sugar
juice of 1 small orange

for the custard
1 vanilla pod, split and deseeded
275ml milk
25g caster sugar
3 small eggs
275g double cream

For the rhubarb: Preheat the oven to 160°C (gas mark 2.5). Remove the leaves and trim the ends of the rhubarb, then wash it and cut it into 1cm pieces. In an ovenproof dish, layer the rhubarb pieces with the sugar. Pour the orange juice over the fruit and sugar and, with the lid on, cook the rhubarb in the oven for 1 hour or until just soft. Remove the rhubarb from the oven and leave it to cool.

For the custard: Put all ingredients, except the double cream, into a pan, whisk them together and cook over a gentle head until the mixture thickens and coats the back of a wooden spoon. (As an alternative, good custard can be purchased in your supermarket.) Whip the cream into soft peaks and then fold it into the custard.

Without putting too much of the rhubarb juice in, put alternate layers of the cooled rhubarb and the creamy custard into 4 tall wine galsses or glass ramekins. This is best served immediately.

Sutherland

The Loft Restaurant

Blair Atholl

DANIEL RICHARDSON

Just off the main road in the village of Blair Atholl is the attractive restaurant and bistro which comprise The Loft. It is an enigmatic place and the welcome, atmosphere and décor – from the cosy sitting-room with its fire for pre-dinner drinks or post-dinner coffee, to the calm, stylish dining-room, to the simple Bistro – are just perfect.

But it is the food that is simply outstanding, stunning in its quality, its presentation, in its every aspect. And the extraordinary thing about The Loft is that the genius in the kitchen is so young. Daniel Richardson, the son of the owner, is only sixteen, yet so utterly focused is he on his career as a chef that he was given special dispensation to leave school early because there was no doubt whatever about his future. At the age of twelve he was a finalist in Junior Masterchef, and he has spent his every spare moment ever since in the kitchen at The Loft. In the Spring of 2002 Daniel reached the final of the Scottish Salmon Young Chef of the Year, a competition open to chefs up to the age of twenty-four, and he was also a Young Chef finalist in the Scottish Chefs award.

Daniel is passionate about produce, cooking and service. He sources the very best produce – game and venison from Pitlochry Game, locally grown fruit and vegetables, cheese from Ian Mellis in Edinburgh, wild mushrooms picked in the woods around Blair Atholl. Lucky indeed are the people who live in the vicinity of Blair Atholl to have a restaurant of the calibre of The Loft in their vicinity.

THE LOFT RESTAURANT

Starter

Pan-fried West Coast scallops
with sauce vierge and a salad of rocket

Wine suggestion: Riesling, 2000, Selaks Estate,
Marlborough (New Zealand)

Main course

Braised fillet of brill
with clams and Scottish girolles and served
with braised cabbage

Wine suggestion: Grüner Veltliner, 1998,
Smaragd, Freie Weingärtner, Wachau (Austria)

Dessert

Fondant of chocolate

Wine suggestion: Late Harvest Riesling, Château
des Charmes, Ontario (Canada)

Menu

Pan-fried West Coast scallops
with sauce vierge and a salad of rocket

This dish is deceptively simple to cook – all you need to do is find the very best produce and do as little as possible to it. You really will be well rewarded.

for the scallops
12 large hand-dived scallops
75ml extra virgin olive oil
sea salt and freshly ground white
    pepper

for the sauce vierge
8 plum tomatoes
150ml extra virgin olive oil
juice of $^1/_2$ a lemon
sea salt and freshly ground white
    pepper

10g fresh basil leaves, finely chopped
10g fresh chives, cut into 2cm lengths
10g fresh chervil, chopped and stems
    removed
5g fresh tarragon, chopped and stems
    removed
1 tbsp aged balsamic vinegar

for the salad
50g rocket leaves, washed and dried

For the scallops: The scallops that you buy must be in their shells and these must be tightly closed. Ask your fishmonger to open them in front of you. When you get them home, remove the roe and the skirt around the scallops and wash them very briefly under cold running water. Place the washed scallops on some kitchen paper on a plate and allow them to dry. It is important to make sure they are quite dry as this will help to seal in all the juices when you cook them. Cut the dry scallops in half. Place a suitable non-stick pan on a high heat, and when it is hot add a little olive oil. Now add the scallops to the pan, cut side down, and season them with the salt and pepper. Cook the scallops for 10–20 seconds on each side – any more and they will become tough.

For the sauce vierge: De-eye and score the bottom of the tomatoes and plunge them into a pan of boiling water for 10 seconds. Remove the tomatoes immediately and plunge them straight into some iced water to prevent them cooking any more. Remove the skins and cut them into quarters. Remove the seeds and place the tomato pieces on some kitchen paper to drain. When the tomato quarters are dry, cut them into uniform squares – this is called tomato concasse. Pour the olive oil into a small pan and warm it gently on the stove. Add the tomato concasse to the pan along with the scallops and a squeeze of lemon juice. Then season with a little salt and pepper, remove the scallops from the pan and again place them on some kitchen paper. Now add the herbs and the balsamic vinegar to the pan and allow the sauce to cook for a further minute.

To serve, pour a little of the remaining olive oil on to the centres of 4 warmed serving plates. Spread the sauce vierge evenly on top of this. Place 6 scallop halves on to each plate in no real order so that it looks quite rustic. Intersperse some of the rocket between each of the scallops and serve at once.

Braised fillet of brill

with clams and Scottish girolles and served
with braised cabbage

I have chosen the following dish to highlight the very essence of Scottish produce.
It is cooked very simply in a 'one-pot' method to maximize flavours.

for the fillet of brill
25ml olive oil
4 x 175g brill fillets
salt and freshly ground black pepper
1 tsp unsalted butter
55ml Madeira
165ml fish stock

for the braised cabbage
225g savoy cabbage
50g unsalted butter
salt and freshly ground black pepper

for the clams and girolles
450g live clams
175g small Scottish girolles
    (chanterelles or St George are also
    fine)
55ml double cream
110g unsalted butter, cut into small
    pieces
1 tbsp fresh chives, finely chopped

for the asparagus
1 bunch of fine asparagus
salted water

For the fillets of brill: Preheat the oven to 180°C (gas mark 4). Ask your
fishmonger to give you 4 prepared brill fillets of equal size that are completely
free of skin and bones. If you cannot get brill, then another flat fish, such as
turbot or sole, could be used. Place a suitably large ovenproof pan on the stove.
Pour in the olive oil and allow it to get hot. Put the fillets in the pan and season
them with salt and pepper. Add the teaspoon of butter at this point – it will help
to brown the fish. When the fish starts to colour, add the Madeira and reduce the
volume by half. Now add the fish stock, put a lid on the pan and place it in the
hot oven. After the fish has been cooking for 6 minutes, remove the pan from the
oven and place it on the top of the stove. Remove the fish from the liquor
(reserving this for later), place it on a plate and cover it with cling film.

For the braised cabbage: Discard the outer leaves of the cabbage. Peel away the
layers, wash them thoroughly and remove the stalks. Dry the leaves off on some
kitchen paper. Now, with a nice sharp knife, shred the leaves into fine strips. Put
the shredded cabbage in a pan with the butter, season it with salt and pepper and
cover it with a lid. This will take about 5–6 minutes to cook. Keep an eye on the

cabbage, stirring it occasionally so it does not burn. It should be kept just a little underdone to emphasise its flavour.

For the clams and girolles: Wash the clams under plenty of cold running water. If any are open, discard them as this indicates that they are dead. If you cannot get clams, you could substitute them with mussels. Scrape the stems of the girolles with a knife and then wash quickly under cold running water. Do not leave them to stand in the water – they will absorb water and lose their flavour. Dry the mushrooms on some kitchen paper. While the cabbage is cooking, bring the reserved fish liquor back to the boil and add the clams and girolles. These will take about 2 minutes to cook. Once all of the clams are open, turn down the heat. Now add the double cream, bring everything to the boil again, add the butter and shake the pan until all of it is incorporated into the sauce. Check the seasoning and adjust if necessary before adding the chopped chives.

For the asparagus: Peel the asparagus, cook it in boiling salted water for 3–4 minutes and then plunge it into ice cold water. Leave it for a couple of minutes, then remove it and drain it on kitchen paper.

To serve, remove the cabbage from the pan, draining any excess liquid from it. Put some cabbage in the centre of each of the 4 serving plates and place a brill fillet on top. Warm the asparagus in a little hot water with a little knob of butter and some salt and pepper. Divide the clams and girolles equally between the 4 plates and place the warmed asparagus spears on top. Pour the sauce around the fish and serve at once.

Fondant of chocolate

The dessert I have chosen to finish with is one of my personal favourites. Its deliciously runny centre is a surprise every time! It is also very simple to make but the result is fabulous.

for the fondant of chocolate
90g dark bitter chocolate
100g unsalted butter
2 whole eggs
2 egg yolks
150g caster sugar
50g plain flour
a little softened butter

for the garnish
a little icing sugar
some whipped double cream or 4
    scoops of good quality vanilla ice
    cream

For the fondant of chocolate: Put the chocolate and the butter into a metal bowl that is sitting over a pan of simmering water. You want the chocolate to melt without allowing it to get too hot. While the chocolate is melting give it an occasional stir. At the same time, put the eggs, the egg yolks and the sugar in a food mixer and whisk until all of the sugar is dissolved. Then gently add the flour to the egg and sugar mixture. By this time all of the chocolate and the butter should be melted. Incorporate the chocolate mixture into the egg mixture and mix in well.

Preheat the oven at 190°C (gas mark 5). To cook this dessert, you will need to use small ovenproof dishes like individual pie moulds. Brush the interior of the mould with softened butter and put a little disc of greaseproof paper at the bottom to prevent the mixture from sticking. Pour the chocolate mixture into the moulds until they are about half to three-quarters full. Put the moulds on an oven tray and cook for 12 minutes. Remove them from the oven and allow them to stand for 30 seconds.

To serve, tip the moulds upside down on to each of the 4 serving plates. Remove the greaseproof paper from the top of the fondants and dust them with icing sugar. When you cut into them, they should still have a nice liquid chocolate centre. Serve them with the cream or vanilla ice cream.

Near Loch Eriboll, Sutherland

North by North West, Pool House

Poolewe

PETER AND MARGARET HARRISON

Peter and Margaret Harrison own and run Pool House together with their daughters, Elizabeth and Mhairi, and Mhairi's husband, John, who is the chef.

Pool House was the home of Osgood MacKenzie, who planned the famous Inverewe gardens (now owned by the National Trust for Scotland) which are just across the bay from them. In the eleven years since the Harrisons bought the house, they have completely renovated it from top to bottom. It is unique in that it has four bedroom suites of such intricate and varied detail and design, each one exceptional in its colours, upholstery and wonderful bathroom fittings. And they all have fantastic views across the bay and to the hills beyond. However, special mention must be made of the Titanic Suite. Mrs Harrison's father was related to the captain of the *Titanic* and the extremely handsome wall lamps are exact replicas of those on the ship – they were even made from the same moulds. There are also artefacts on the wall from Harland and Wolff, the Belfast-based shipbuilders who built the great ship, and the attention to fascinating detail in this (and in all the other suites) is most impressive. For sheer comfort nothing could beat them.

Downstairs, the handsome, comfortable book-filled drawing room has a large fireplace. There is a small dining room, which is ideal for private parties, and the main dining room is absolutely stunning. It was decorated by the Harrison's artistic daughter, Elizabeth, and it features a huge compass on the end, facing the sea, with tiny stars (all hand painted) on the ceiling. The room is a shade of blue that captures the nautical theme but it still manages to be warm. The tables are beautiful, with white napery and flowers. And the food is, quite simply, delicious.

Their shellfish is bought locally, mostly from Mark Wiseman. The fish is from Kinlochbervie and the smoked salmon is from the Aultbea smokehouse. The Harrison's buy their meat from Donald Russell, and their wines from Corney and Barrow.

To eat in such a setting as the Pool House dining room, with its lovely views and unique décor, is a real pleasure and the warmth of welcome the Harrisons exude is an example of hospitality at its best.

NORTH BY NORTH WEST, POOL HOUSE

Starter

Pan-fried wood pigeon
on a bed of risotto with a game sauce

Wine suggestion: Beaune 1èr Cru VSR, Chanson,
Burgundy (France) or Les Terrasses, 1999,
Bodega Alvaro Palacios, Priorato (Spain)

Main course

Pan-seared scallops with lobster sauce,
creamed garlic and herb mash and
asparagus

Wine suggestion: Vaucoupin, 1998, Chablis 1èr
Cru, Chanson, Burgundy (France)

Dessert

Glazed lemon flan

Wine suggestion: Château de Malle, Sauternes
2ème Cru, 1995, Bordeaux (France)

Pan-fried wood pigeon
on a bed of risotto with a game sauce

To save you having too much to do on the day you serve this dish, you could make both the game sauce and the chicken stock the day before.

for the game sauce
2 wood pigeon carcasses
2 tbsp olive oil
3 sprigs of fresh thyme
2 carrots, roughly chopped
1 head of garlic, cut in half
2 tbsp tomato purée
1 stick of celery, roughly chopped
1^1/$_2$ litre water
250ml port

for the chicken stock
chicken pieces, e.g. 1 carcass, plus 2
    drumsticks and 2 wings
2 medium carrots, peeled and chopped
1 medium onion, peeled and chopped
2 medium sticks of celery, chopped
2 sprigs of fresh thyme
a handful of fresh parsley
2 litre water

for the risotto
175g smoked streaky bacon, chopped
2 shallots, finely chopped
50g unsalted butter clarified
2 cloves of garlic, crushed
200g Arborio rice
chicken stock
1 sprig of fresh rosemary, picked

for the wood pigeon
4 wood pigeon breasts (ask your
    butcher to bone 2 birds, reserving
    the carcasses for the stock)
salt and freshly ground black pepper
a little olive oil and a knob of butter,
    for frying

for the garnish
a few sprigs of fresh chervil

For the game sauce: Brown the wood pigeon carcasses in the olive oil on a high heat for approximately 4–5 minutes. Next, add all the other ingredients, except the port, and allow the liquid to simmer for 1 hour. Strain, add the port and cook the liquid until it is reduced by about half before re-straining the sauce.

For the chicken stock: Put all the ingredients into a pot and bring them to the boil. Simmer the stock for 1–1^1/$_2$ hours until there is about ^{1}/$_2$ litre left and then strain it.

For the risotto: Fry the bacon and shallots in the butter over a medium heat for 4–5 minutes, then add the garlic and rice and fry for a further minute until the rice grains are well coated in butter. Add enough chicken stock to cover the rice. Once it has come to the boil, keep stirring and gradually add more stock, a ladleful at a time, until it has been absorbed. When the rice is soft to bite, add the rosemary, remove the pan from the heat and start to prepare the wood pigeon. At this stage, the rice should be moist but not soupy.

For the wood pigeon: Season the breasts with salt and pepper. Add a little olive oil and a knob of butter to a frying pan and, when this is sizzling, add the wood pigeon breasts, skin side down, and cook for $2^1/_2$ minutes. Turn the breasts and lower the heat. Cook for a further 2–3 minutes (longer if you prefer them well done), then remove them and allow them to rest on a plate or board for several minutes.

To serve, warm up the risotto in the pan (adding a little more stock if you think the consistency is too thick) and season it to taste. Place a mound of risotto in the centre of each of the 4 serving plates and place a wood pigeon breast on top of it. If you have made the game sauce in advance, warm it through. Drizzle some game sauce around the outside of the risotto and garnish the dish with the chervil.

Pan-seared scallops

with lobster sauce, creamed garlic and herb mash
and asparagus

I chose this dish as, here at Poolewe, we get the most fantastic diver-caught scallops (the biggest being 500g in the shell) from the loch in front of the hotel. However, a good fishmonger will be able to get you quality scallops. I have cheated and saved time by using a tin of lobster bisque but you can make your own sauce if you prefer.

for the asparagus
450g fresh asparagus
salted water

for the garlic and herb mash
1.125kg waxy potatoes, peeled and cut
   into chunks
salted water
150ml double cream
2 tbsp fresh herbs (any combination
   will do), chopped
4 cloves of garlic, finely chopped
25g unsalted butter
30ml olive oil
salt and freshly ground pepper

for the pan-seared scallops
12 good-sized scallops (preferably
   diver-caught)
a little olive oil
1 tbsp unsalted butter

for the lobster sauce
75ml sweet sherry or Marsala
1 tin of Baxter's lobster bisque

for the garnish
a few sprigs of fresh chervil

For the asparagus: Peel the asparagus with a potato peeler, going from the base of the tip down to the root but only taking the minimum away or you will be left with very thin stems. Plunge them into boiling salted water for 30 seconds and then refresh them in cold water, until they are chilled.

For the garlic and herb mash: Boil the peeled potatoes in the salted water until they are soft. Now drain the potatoes in a colander and leave them to steam while you prepare the cream. Put the cream, herbs and garlic into a pan and bring them to the boil. Add the potatoes, butter and olive oil and keep stirring over a low heat for approximately $1^1/_2$–2 minutes. Then tip the mixture into a colander to drain before putting the potato mixture into a food processor and blitzing it. Season the mash with salt and pepper to taste and keep it warm while you cook the scallops.

For the pan-seared scallops: Put the frying pan on a high heat with just enough olive oil to give a very light coating. When the oil is hot, season the scallops and place them in the pan. They should really sizzle. Cook the scallops on each side for approximately 1 minute until they have a good colour (the time will vary according to their size). Remove them from the heat and put them on a plate under a low grill or in a warm oven. Add the butter to the same pan and, when it is hot, put in the asparagus to glaze and reheat it. Then place the cooked asparagus with the scallops.

For the lobster sauce: Add the sherry or Marsala to the pan that the scallops and asparagus were cooked in. Deglaze the pan, then pour in the tin of lobster bisque and bring it to the boil. Remove the sauce from the heat and strain the contents into a small pot.

To serve, put some of the garlic mash in the centre of each of the 4 serving plates with the scallops and asparagus on top. Drizzle the sauce over them and garnish the dish with the chervil.

Glazed lemon flan

for the sweet pastry
110g unsalted butter, softened
225g plain flour
75g icing sugar
1 vanilla pod, split lengthways and
   seeds removed and reserved
a small pinch of salt
1 small egg, lightly beaten
a little oil and flour, for greasing

for the filling
4 eggs
150ml double cream
2 lemons – use the rind from one and
   the juice from both
175g caster sugar

for the garnish
a little icing sugar, for dusting
300ml double cream, lightly whipped
fresh raspberries

For the sweet pastry: Put the butter, flour, icing sugar, vanilla pod seeds and salt in a food processor. Turn on the machine to a medium speed and whizz until you have a mixture that resembles fine breadcrumbs. Reduce the speed and slowly and gradually add the lightly beaten egg until the mixture turns into a firm ball of pastry. (You may have a little egg left over.) Wrap the pastry ball in cling film and place it in the fridge to chill for at least 20 minutes. (It can be made the day before and left overnight if you like.) Then, 15 minutes before you need the pastry, remove it from the fridge and allow it to rest. Take an 18cm fluted loose-bottomed flan tin (or you could use 4 individual tins) and grease it well with the oil, ensuring that the fluted sides and base are well covered. Dust the tin with a little flour to prevent the pastry from sticking.

Preheat the oven to 150°C (gas mark 2). Roll the pastry out on a floured surface until it is about 3mm thick and is of sufficient diameter to cover the flan tin. Then carefully, using your rolling pin, lift up the rolled-out pastry and place it over the flan tin. Gently push the pastry into the tin, making sure it goes right into the fluted sides. Carefully run a knife around the top edge to trim off any excess. Prick the pastry all over using a fork. To bake blind, line the pastry with baking parchment and fill the case with ceramic baking beans (if you do not have any, pulses, dried beans or pasta shapes work just as well). This will stop the base of the flan rising and prevent the sides from collapsing. Place the flan tin in the preheated oven for approximately 20 minutes. Remove it and leave it to cool for a few minutes, before carefully removing the blind-baking filling. Do not remove the pastry from the tin.

For the lemon filling: Keep the oven at 150°C (gas mark 2). Place the eggs, double cream, lemon rind and juice and caster sugar in a bowl and whisk thoroughly. Put the mixture in the pastry case or divide it between the individual cases. Put the flan in the oven and bake for approximately for 20–25 minutes for the large case or 10 minutes for the individual ones. The lemon tart should feel soft and spring back when ready. Allow the flan to cool before removing it from the tin. Dust the flan with icing sugar and then place it under a very hot preheated grill so that the sugar browns quickly.

To serve, remove the flan from the grill and slice it into generous wedges. Immediately place a piece of flan on each of the 4 serving plates along with some of the lightly whipped double cream and some fresh raspberries.

Creels, Kylesku, Sutherland

Loch a' Chàirn Bhàin, near Kylesku, Sutherland

Scarista House

Harris

TIM AND PATRICIA MARTIN

Scarista House is an attractive former manse, with a vast sweep of golden sandy beach in front of it. It surely boasts one of the most beautiful views in Scotland. Tim and Patricia Martin live here and run their lovely home as a small hotel. They both knew the area before moving to Harris, having spent many holidays nearby, and when Tim and Patricia, a musician, decided they had had enough of living and working in London, they bought this distinctive white house. It had became a hotel of renown many years earlier, when Andrew and Alison Johnson lived there, and the joy for the many guests who return comes from the fact that it continues to be an excellent place to stay.

Scarista has five bedrooms, a comfortable library downstairs with a welcoming fire, and an elegant dining room. One's first impressions on entering the house are of warmth and comfort. And the food is delicious. Tim cooks more than Patricia and the food they produce is a treat. They use as much local produce as they can get – lobsters come from the bay in front of the house, langoustines and scallops from the Sound of Harris and the wet fish comes from trawlers in Stornoway. Breakfast kippers come from Inverawe Smokehouse in Argyll, their venison is from North Harris or North Uist, and their game – woodcock, snipe and grouse – comes from the estate next-door to them. There are an increasing number of fruit and vegetable growers in South Harris, and Tim and Patricia grow a variety of salad leaves, potatoes and some vegetables themselves, with the help of their gardener. Their excellent cheeses come from Letterfinlay, near Spean Bridge.

Generally speaking, it is hard to beat Scotland for scenery to take one's breath away but Scarista and South Harris leave the visitor with such an impression of unrivalled beauty, an almost magnetic quality, that many are drawn back time and time again. Scarista is a house of peace with all the best ingredients for a perfect holiday – very good food, comfort and warmth. And for those who enjoy walking, there are the wild, deserted beaches.

SCARISTA HOUSE

Starter

Sound of Harris langoustine bisque
with Dijon mayonnaise

Wine suggestion: A good Muscadet-sur-lie or
New Zealand Sauvignon

Main course

Salmi of game birds

Wine suggestion: A good red Burgundy with a
little bit of age, such as our Gevrey-
Chambertin, 1996

Dessert

Pears poached in white wine
with cinnamon, eau de vie de Poire William
cream and cinnamon shortbread

Wine suggestion: A glass of Poire William or a
well botrytised sweet white wine – perhaps a
Jurançon or Monbazillac

Menu

Sound of Harris langoustine bisque

with Dijon mayonnaise

We use langoustines from the Sound of Harris for our bisque, since we get them fresh and live the day they are landed, but frankly by the time they've been made into bisque, with all the other flavours involved, any decent langoustines will taste good. You can also use a big crab or a small 450g lobster instead and you can vary the herbs as well – perhaps using parsley or basil, and leaving out the star anise if you don't want such an aniseed flavour. This quantity makes more than enough for four people as a starter, but you'd probably get through the lot if you weren't having anything else.

for the langoustine bisque
450g langoustines or langoustine
 heads and shells
1 large carrot, diced
1 big leek, thinly sliced
2 large onions, peeled and chopped
2 cloves of garlic, crushed
4 stalks of fresh lovage with leaves,
 chopped
a small bunch of fresh chervil,
 chopped
a small bunch of fresh tarragon,
 chopped
3 tbsp olive oil
2 litres fish stock (readymade is fine)
a pinch of saffron
1 star anise
1 x 400g tin of tomatoes
1 x 142g tin of tomato purée
75ml brandy

$\frac{1}{2}$ bottle white wine
6 drops of Tabasco
50g long grain rice
salt and freshly ground black pepper

for the mayonnaise
2 egg yolks
1 dsp Dijon mustard
salt and freshly ground black pepper
100ml groundnut oil
150ml highly flavoured olive oil (we
 use the oil in which we have
 marinated olives with garlic, chillies
 and herbs, but plain extra virgin will
 be fine)
2 tsp lemon juice

for the garnish
a few strands of saffron

For the langoustine bisque: This soup is not difficult to make but do give yourself plenty of time. If you have bought (or caught) live langoustines, put them in the freezer, wrapped in damp newspaper, to kill them relatively painlessly. Sweat the carrot, leek, onion, garlic and herbs in the olive oil until they are soft. Meanwhile, bring the stock to the boil in a large pan and cook the langoustines in it for about 20 minutes – far longer than if you were going to eat them whole. Drain the langoustines, reserve the stock and put the langoustines back into the pan. Put the pan on a solid surface and bash the langoustines to a pulp with the end of a wooden rolling pin or something similar. Add the cooked herbs and vegetables and the saffron, star anise, tinned tomatoes and tomato purée to the pan with the crushed langoustines. Mix everything together and then pour in the brandy. Reduce the liquid over a high heat until there is only a little of it left and then do the same with the white wine. Now pour the reserved stock back into the pan, adding the rice and Tabasco, and simmer the bisque for about half an hour until the rice is very well cooked. If you can find the star anise, take out it. Next comes the tedious and messy part. Blitz the soup in a liquidiser, a little at a time, and then push it through a coarse sieve or Mouli. Season the soup, taste it and add some more Tabasco or a little more brandy if you think it needs it.

For the Dijon mayonnaise: In a large bowl, whisk together the egg yolks and mustard with a little salt and pepper. Slowly add the groundnut oil, whisking as hard as you can. Now do the same with the olive oil to make a nice, glossy mayonnaise and, finally, beat in the lemon juice.

To serve, heat the bisque up again and, when it is good and hot, ladle it into bowls. Add a generous dollop of the Dijon mayonnaise and decorate the bisque with a few saffron strands (no more than 4 or 5 in each bowl).

Salmi of game birds

for the game sauce

4 grouse or mallard, or 6
   woodcock, or a
   combination of birds,
   plucked and dressed

25g unsalted butter

1 carrot, chopped

1 onion, chopped

250ml dry white wine

a sprig of fresh thyme

1 tbsp Madeira or sweet
   sherry

200ml double cream

salt and freshly ground
   black pepper

for the game bird
   breasts

4 or 6 breasts from the
   half-roasted game birds

50g unsalted butter

75ml cognac

for the accompaniments

a mixture of boiled wild
   and basmati rice

oven-roasted courgettes
   and onions

For the game sauce: Preheat the oven to 250°C (gas mark 9). Place the birds in a roasting pan with the butter and half-roast them in the hot oven for 15 minutes. Allow them to become cool enough to handle, slice off the breasts and set these aside in the fridge. Roughly chop the carcasses, put them back in the roasting pan in the hot oven and brown them – expect this to take about 25 minutes. Add the carrot and onion and roast for another 5 minutes. Remove the bones and vegetables from the roasting pan and transfer them to a saucepan. Put the roasting pan on top of the stove over a high heat and deglaze it with half of the white wine. Now scrape the contents of the roasting pan into the saucepan with the bones and vegetables in it, add the rest of the wine and reduce the liquid by half. Add the thyme, put in enough water to cover the bones and vegetables and simmer the stock for $1^{1}/_{2}$ hours. Strain the stock into a fresh pan, add the Madeira and reduce it over a high heat until it begins to turn syrupy. Turn off the heat.

For the game bird breasts: Remove the breasts from the fridge and sauté them in the butter over a moderate heat, turning them until they are just pink – a total cooking time of about 5 minutes. Pour the cognac into the pan, light it and then shake the pan until the flames die down.

To serve, add the cream to the stock, boil it for a couple of minutes until the sauce thickens and then season it with the salt and pepper. Place 2 or 3 sautéed breasts on each of the 4 serving plates, pour the sauce around them and immediately present the dish with the rice and courgettes.

Pears poached in white wine

with cinnamon, eau de vie de Poire William cream and cinnamon shortbread

This is a very simple dessert with lovely intense flavours from the wine and eau de vie.

for the eau de vie creams

200ml double cream

150ml milk

30g caster sugar

2 leaves of gelatin, softened in cold
   water

3 tbsp eau de vie de Poire William

for the poached pears

4 pears

50g caster sugar

250ml dry white wine

250ml water

1 cinnamon stick

for the cinnamon shortbread

200g plain flour

100g cornflour

100g caster sugar

250g unsalted butter

1 stick of cinnamon, grated

For the eau de vie creams: Put the double cream, milk and caster sugar into a saucepan. Squeeze the water from the gelatin, add it to the pan and heat the mixture gently until the sugar has dissolved and the gelatin has melted, taking care not to allow it to boil. Remove the pan from the heat and stir in the eau de vie. Pour the mixture into 4 dariole moulds and chill them in the fridge until they have set. Expect this to take about 4 hours.

For the poached pears: Peel the pears and cut a thin slice off the bottoms so that they stand upright. Put the peeled pears into a saucepan with all the other ingredients. Bring everything to the boil and simmer until the pears are tender. The time this takes will depend on the ripeness of the pears. Check this by inserting a blunt knife into them occasionally. Once they are soft, remove them from the liquid and set them aside. Boil the remaining liquid rapidly until it reduces and becomes thick and syrupy.

For the cinnamon shortbread: These quantities will make more than you need for this dish but the dough keeps well in the fridge for several days and it can also be frozen. Alternatively, you could just make a big batch of biscuits to eat anytime. Preheat the oven to 220°C (gas mark 7). Sift the flour and cornflour together, then combine this mixture with all the other ingredients and beat until they come together to form a softish dough. Turn the dough on to a floured board. Cut the dough in half and roll one half of it out thinly until it is about 3mm thick. Using a round pastry cutter about 5cm in diameter, cut out 8 biscuits. Place the biscuits on a greased baking sheet and bake them in the oven for about 5–10 minutes. Remove them and, while they are still hot, sprinkle them with caster sugar and grate a dusting of cinnamon over them. Leave the biscuits on a wire rack to cool.

To serve, dip the dariole moulds into hot water for a few seconds, turn them upside down over the serving plates and give them a shake until the cream puddings come out. If they don't drop out immediately, you might need to dip them in hot water again but don't leave them in the water for too long. Stand a poached pear upright next to each cream, spoon over some of the cooking syrup from the pears and finally add a cinnamon shortbread biscuit.

Luskentyre, Isle of Harris

The Carnegie Club, Skibo Castle

Dornoch

CRAIG ROWLAND

The wonderful castle of Skibo – which was built during the 1200s for Bishop Gilbert of Dornoch, was extended and sumptuously modernised by the great philanthropist Andrew Carnegie in Edwardian times, and which is now the centre of the Carnegie Club, having been bought and lovingly restored by Peter de Savary in 1990 – stands in 7,500 acres of enchanting land. This comprises the extensive and beautiful gardens which surround the castle, farmland, moorland and two golf courses.

Skibo lies in a microclimate, which accounts for the lushness of the gardens. It also enjoys an extraordinarily low rainfall. The gardens produce much of the fruit and vegetables used by Head Chef Craig Rowland and his team of nine chefs and assistants in the vast kitchen for the guests at Skibo. Although it is a club, anyone can stay there once before becoming a member, and the daily charges include food, wines and many of the sporting activities on offer at the estate. Most notably, this means golf but guests can also enjoy falconry, riding, tennis, sporting clays, 4x4 off-road driving and swimming in the beautiful pool in the pavilion, which was one of Andrew Carnegie's creations – and it is so magnificent that it justifies being so described!

The castle is filled with furniture, antiques and *objets d'art* that belonged to the Carnegie family. Within the immaculately kept grounds are twelve lodges, each consisting of between one and five bedrooms. And all the lodges are just as beautifully and comfortably decorated and upholstered as the castle itself.

Skibo has hosted many special events for very many well-known individuals, who know that they can rely on complete privacy within the estate environs. But what makes Skibo so special is the fact that it does not feel like a hotel, partly because it isn't one but chiefly because, despite the splendour and the magnificence of the interior and exterior, the staff and all who are responsible for making Skibo worthy of its reputation are not at all remote and excessively formal. There is an air of welcome and attention to personal and individual needs which creates such a very relaxing atmosphere.

THE CARNEGIE CLUB
SKIBO CASTLE

Starter

Pigeon consommé
with foie gras wontons

Wine suggestion: Malmsey Quinta do Serrada,
1830 (Madeira)

Main course

Turbot with braised chicory

Wine suggestion: Grand Cru Vaudésir, 1997,
Chablis, Domaine Joseph Drouhin (France)

Dessert

Citrus fruit tartlets with glazed sabayon

Wine suggestion: Cru Barréjats, 1995,
Barsac (France)

Menu

Pigeon consommé
with foie gras wontons

for the game stock
2 pigeon carcasses
2 carrots, peeled and
    chopped
2 sticks of celery,
    chopped
4 onions, peeled and
    chopped
2 bay leaves
1.5 litres water

for the consommé
1.2 litres of the game
    stock, chilled
1 chicken breast, minced
2 carrots, peeled and
    finely chopped

2 sticks of celery, finely
    chopped
2 leeks, finely chopped
3 sprigs of fresh thyme
75ml port
salt and white pepper
4 egg whites

for the wontons
50g ceps, dried
1 foie gras lobe, cut into
    4 thumbnail-size
    pieces
55ml water
50g cornflour
4 sheets of wonton
    pastry, shop bought

for the pigeon breasts
2 pigeon breasts
a little oil and butter,
    for sautéing

for the
    accompaniments
4 quail eggs, softly
    poached
2 tsp flat-leaf parsley,
    chopped
12 whole tarragon
    leaves
16 chanterelles, pan-
    fried in a little butter
55ml truffle oil

For the game stock: Put all the ingredients into a large pan, bring everything to the boil, reduce the heat to a simmer and cook for 3 hours. Strain the stock, leave it to cool and chill it in the fridge.

For the consommé: Put the chilled game stock into a 4-litre saucepan and thoroughly mix in all the ingredients – these will be used for clarifying the stock. Put the pan on a low heat and stir gently until the clarifying ingredients rise and form a 'raft' over the entire surface of the liquid. Once this stage has been reached, it is very important not to stir the mixture again. Continue to simmer gently for 10 minutes, ensuring no breaks appear in the raft. Turn off the heat. Carefully make a hole in the raft with the back of a ladle, trying not to disrupt it too much. Gently spoon out the clarified liquid through the hole and then strain it through a muslin cloth, discarding the clarifying ingredients.

For the wontons: Put the dried ceps into a coffee grinder, grind them to a powder and then roll the foie gras pieces in this to coat them. Mix the water and cornflour together and use the mixture to moisten the wonton pastry. Place a piece of cep-coated foie gras in the centre of each wonton pastry square, draw the edges up and press them together to form little frilly-topped parcels. Deep-fry the foie gras wontons at 160°C for 1 minute.

For the pigeon breasts: Sauté the pigeon breasts in the oil and butter for $1^1/_2$ minutes on each side. The breasts should not be overcooked and the meat should remain nice and pink. Remove the breasts from the pan and allow them to rest at room temperature for 2 minutes before slicing them.

To serve, ladle the hot consommé into 4 serving bowls or cups. Divide up the accompaniments between them, arranging them neatly in the soup and floating a wonton on the surface. Finally, add a few drops of truffle oil, which will also float on the soup.

Turbot
with braised chicory

for the braised chicory
4 heads of chicory, halved
30ml olive oil
a pinch of caster sugar
salt and white pepper
500ml chicken stock (readymade is fine)

for the turbot
4 x 200g turbot fillets
24 thin slices of pancetta
15ml olive oil

for the peas
300g fresh or frozen garden peas
150g Kasseler (a type of German
  smoked ham), diced into pea-sized
  cubes

30ml olive oil
100g unsalted butter
100ml double cream
30ml balsamic vinegar
salt and freshly ground white pepper

for the sauce
$^1/_2$ bottle of red Burgundy
2 shallots, peeled and chopped
2 sprigs of fresh thyme
570ml fish stock (readymade is fine)

for the deep-fried parsley
50g flat-leaf parsley, picked
sunflower oil, for deep-frying

For the braised chicory: Fry the chicory halves in a hot pan with the olive oil, sugar, salt and pepper. Brown it on all sides and then cover it with the chicken stock. Reduce the heat and cook until the stock has evaporated and the chicory is tender. Expect this to take about 20 minutes.

For the turbot: Trim the turbot fillets neatly so that they are roughly the size of the palm of your hand. Neatly arrange the slices of pancetta on one side of each fillet, overlapping them slightly. Pan-fry the fish, pancetta side down, in the olive oil over a medium heat for 2 minutes on each side.

For the peas: Boil the fresh or frozen peas until they are cooked. Fry the Kasseler in the olive oil over a high heat for about 2 minutes, until it is nicely browned. Add the balsamic vinegar, double cream and butter and continue to cook, stirring continuously, until it has reduced to a sauce-like consistency. Then add the cooked peas and season.

For the sauce: Put the red wine, shallots and thyme into a pan and, over a high heat, reduce the liquid down to a glaze. Add the fish stock and continue to cook until it has reduced by half. Remove the sauce from the heat and strain it. Heat the sauce up again before serving.

For the deep-fried parsley: Deep-fry the parsley at 160°C for 30 seconds. Drain it on kitchen paper, allow it to cool and divide it into 20 little piles.

To serve, spoon the pea mixture around the rims of the 4 serving plates to form a border and put 5 small piles of deep-fried parsley at evenly spaced intervals on top. In the centre of each plate, place some of the braised chicory with a turbot fillet on top, and serve with the sauce reduction.

Citrus fruit tartlets

with glazed sabayon

for the shortbread pastry
50g unsalted butter, softened
$1/2$ an egg, lightly beaten
zest of $1/2$ a lemon
25g caster sugar
80g plain flour
20g ground almonds

for the citrus fruit confit
1 orange
1 pink grapefruit
1 lime
150g caster sugar
150ml water

1 sprig of fresh thyme
1 sprig of fresh rosemary

for the sabayon
4 egg yolks
1 egg
half of the fruit syrup from the confit

for the caramel cages
150g caster sugar
150ml water

for the garnish
some dark chocolate drops
a little blue curaçao

For the shortbread pastry: Preheat the oven to 160°C (gas mark 2.5). Mix together the softened butter, egg, lemon zest and sugar. Fold in the flour and almonds and mix to form a soft paste. Roll the paste out to a thickness of about 0.5cm. Line 4 individual greased tartlet moulds with the paste, put a layer of greaseproof paper topped with ceramic baking beans (dried beans or pasta shapes will work just as well) on top and bake blind for 15 minutes. This method of baking stops the base rising and also prevents the sides from collapsing.

For the citrus fruit confit: Squeeze the juice from the citrus fruits. Remove the rinds, segment the squeezed fruits and place all the segments in a shallow dish. Put the sugar into a saucepan with a little water and, over a high heat, bring the mixture to a temperature of 165°C (use a sugar thermometer to check the temperature) and cook until a caramel forms. Add the citrus juice to this pan, along with the thyme and rosemary. Bring everything to the boil and cook for 5 minutes. Pour the hot liquid over the segments, cover and allow the segments to steep in the fridge overnight.

For the sabayon: Put all the ingredients into a mixing bowl, place the bowl over a pan of hot water and whisk them together until the mixture thickens and becomes frothy.

For the caramel cages: Make a caramel using the same method as you used for the caramel in the fruit confit. Lightly grease the outside of a ladle and drizzle the hot caramel over it, forming a criss-cross pattern. When the caramel has hardened slightly, carefully remove it and repeat for the other 3 cages.

To serve, fan the steeped fruit segments out over the bases of the tartlets and pour the sabayon over them. Dot the chocolate drops over the surface and put the tartlets under a hot grill until they are golden brown and glazed. Place a tartlet on each of the 4 serving plates. Mix the remainder of the syrup with the blue curaçao, drizzle the liquid around the tartlets and top each with a caramel cage.

Italian Chapel, Orkney

Summer Isles Hotel

Achiltibuie

MARK AND GERRY IRVINE

Mark and Gerry Irvine took over the Summer Isles Hotel from Mark's father, Robert, eighteen years ago. Their search for a chef led to a chance meeting with Chris Firth-Bernard in Cambridge and they offered him a rather tenuous life here. Chris has been a chef since the age of sixteen but he was, and still is, a keen ornithologist and naturalist, and he accepted. This was the start of a really fantastic team of people, and the very atmosphere at the Summer Isles reflects the success that a first-rate team of dedicated people can produce.

The exterior of the long, low, white hotel consists of a main house with skilfully and elegantly converted cottages beside it. Inside and out, there are bleached stones from the beach displayed in glass vases and in rows on the windowsill, Gerry Irvine's lovely paintings hang on the walls and there is a general air of sophisticated comfort in all the rooms. And oh the food! Chris is an inspired chef. He has always been passionate about fish, all of which is obtained from David Mackay in nearby Lochinver, and you can watch the local boats bringing in the shellfish catch from the comfort of the dining room. He lets the excellence of the ingredients speak for themselves, and it is no surprise that he was awarded a Michelin star in 1998. Terrific though his meat and fish courses are (he buys his meat from the first-rate butcher, Duncan Fraser in Inverness), so too are the contents of the pudding trolley. And the cheese trolley, containing some fourteen cheeses of Scottish and French origin with a selection of port to accompany them, is magnificent. The wine list is also so very impressive. This is Mark's domain and he works on it during the winter months when the hotel is closed.

Summer Isles Hotel is a unique, luxurious establishment, which combines a great welcome with its attention to detail to create a truly exceptional experience.

SUMMER ISLES HOTEL

Starter

Smoked haddock flan

Wine suggestion: Pouilly Fumé, 2000, Serge
Dagueneau (France)

Main course

Summer Isles lobster
with herbs and a vermouth butter sauce

Wine suggestion: Mâcon Clessé, 1996, Domaine
de la Bongran, Jean Thevenet (France)

Dessert

Fried bananas and lime
with a butterscotch sauce

Wine suggestion: Pedro Ximenez, San Emilio,
Emilio Lustau, Jerez, N.V. (Spain)

Menu

Smoked haddock flan

for the flan case
225g plain flour
120g unsalted butter
1 egg yolk
2 tbsp cold water
a pinch of salt

for the smoked haddock filling
6 bay leaves
12 peppercorns
500ml milk
450g undyed smoked haddock

30g unsalted butter
30g plain flour
100ml double cream
3 large free-range eggs
15ml sunflower oil
1 small onion, finely chopped

for the garnish
a little warm melted butter
freshly ground black pepper
a few chives, snipped

For the flan case: Preheat the oven to 190°C (gas mark 5). Rub the butter and salt into the flour until it resembles coarse breadcrumbs. Combine the egg yolk with the water and mix this into the butter and flour mixture to form a smooth dough. Wrap the dough in cling film and chill it in the fridge for at least 30 minutes. Grease a loose-bottomed 20cm flan ring and line it with the pastry. Put a layer of baking parchment over the pastry, top with ceramic baking beans (dried butter beans or similar will work just as well) and bake blind for 20 minutes – this will stop the base rising and prevent the sides from collapsing. Remove the pastry case from the oven, discard the baking beans and parchment but leave the pastry in the flan ring until it has cooled completely.

For the smoked haddock filling: Put the bay leaves, peppercorns and milk in a large saucepan and poach the haddock in this for 5 minutes. Remove the fish and place it on one side, straining and reserving the liquid. In a small saucepan gently melt the butter. Incorporate the flour to form a soft ball and leave this to cool slightly before gradually adding the reserved liquor, beating each time you add some until the mixture becomes smooth. At this stage, you should have used about 300ml of the reserved haddock liquid. Set the sauce aside to cool again. Now add the cream, eggs and a further 100ml of the reserved milk.

Preheat the oven to 190°C (gas mark 5). Heat up a small frying pan and add the sunflower oil. When it is hot, add the onion to the pan and sauté it until it becomes slightly brown. Line the pastry base with the sautéed onion. Skin the fish, break it up and cover the onions with it. Finally pour the haddock velouté (sauce) over the fish and bake the flan for around 30 minutes until the filling is set.

To serve, place a wedge of flan on each of the 4 serving plates with some warm melted butter, a grinding of black pepper and a scattering of snipped chives.

Summer Isles lobster
with herbs and a vermouth butter sauce

for the lobsters
2 x 750g lobsters

for the vermouth butter sauce
570ml fish stock (readymade is fine)
75ml vermouth
110g unsalted butter

for the garnish
1 sprig of fresh dill
1 sprig of fresh tarragon

1 sprig of fresh flat-leaf parsley
a small handful of fresh basil leaves,
  shredded

for the accompaniments
boiled, minted new potatoes
asparagus spears
hollandaise sauce

For the lobsters: Boil the lobsters in plenty of salted water for 10 minutes. Remove the lobsters from the water and allow them to cool but do not refrigerate them. When cool, separate the tails from the heads. Carefully split each lobster in half lengthways and remove all the flesh from the tails and claws. Make some angled slices through each tailpiece and arrange the 4 halves on a buttered tray. Heat the lobster pieces under a hot grill for 30 seconds and then put them to rest on a warm plate.

For the vermouth butter sauce: Heat the fish stock over a high heat until it has reduced to about half a cup. Then add the vermouth and reduce further until you have approximately 55ml of liquid. Now stir the butter into the fish reduction. Allow the butter to melt but do not boil the sauce.

To serve, place a half lobster on each plate with a trickle of the sauce and arrange the herbs around it. Present the dish with boiled, minted new potatoes and asparagus spears with hollandaise sauce.

Fried bananas and lime

with a butterscotch sauce

for the butterscotch sauce
50g unsalted butter
50g soft brown sugar
30ml golden syrup
200g evaporated milk
100ml double cream

for the fried bananas
a few drops of sunflower oil
4 slightly under-ripe bananas, peeled
    and cut in half lengthways
zest of 1 lime
2 tsp caster sugar

For the butterscotch sauce: Combine the butter, sugar and golden syrup in a small pan over a low heat and cook until the sugar has dissolved. Add the evaporated milk and cream and simmer for 2 minutes.

For the fried bananas: Heat the sunflower oil in a heavy-based frying pan. Add the bananas and cook them for about 3 minutes, until they are brown on one side. Add the lime zest and sprinkle in the sugar. Turn the bananas and cook them on the other side again until they are brown.

To serve, place two banana halves on each of the 4 serving plates and drizzle the butterscotch sauce around them.

Loch Sligachan, Isle of Skye

Weights, measures and servings

All weights, measures and servings are approximate conversions.

SOLID WEIGHT CONVERSIONS

Metric	Imperial
10g	$^1/_2$ oz
20g	$^3/_4$ oz
25g	1 oz
40g	$1^1/_2$ oz
50g	2 oz
60g	$2^1/_2$ oz
75g	3 oz
110g	4oz
125g	$4^1/_2$ oz
150g	5 oz
175g	6 oz
200g	7 oz
225g	8 oz
250g	9 oz
275g	10 oz
350g	12 oz
450g	1 lb
700g	$1^1/_2$ lb
900g	2 lb
1.35 kg	3 lb

STANDARDS SOLID

1 oz	=	25g
1 lb	=	16 oz
1 g	=	0.35 oz
1 kg	=	2.2 lb

LIQUID CONVERSIONS

Metric	Imperial
55ml	2 fl.oz
75ml	3 fl.oz
150ml	5 fl.oz ($^1/_4$ pint)
275ml	$^1/_2$ pint
425ml	$^3/_4$ pint
570ml	1 pint
725ml	$1^1/_2$ pints
1 litre	$1^3/_4$ pints
1.2 litre	2 pints
1.5 litre	$2^1/_2$ pints
2.25 litre	4 pints

STANDARDS LIQUID

1tsp	=	5ml
1 tbsp	=	15ml
1 fl.oz	=	30ml
1 pint	=	20 fl.oz
1 litre	=	35 fl.oz

OVEN TEMPERATURE CONVERSIONS

°C	Gas	°F
140	1	275
150	2	300
170	3	325
180	4	350
190	5	375
200	6	400
220	7	425
230	8	450
240	9	475

Contributor details

2 Quail
Castle Street
Dornoch IV25 3SN
01862 811811

Ackergill Tower
By Wick
Caithness KW1 4RG
01955 603556

The House of Bruar
By Blair Atholl
Perthshire PH18 5TW
01796 483236

Café One
75 Castle Street
Inverness IV2 3EA
01463 226200

The Ceilidh Place
14 West Argyle Street
Ullapool IV26 2TY
01854 612103

Clifton House
Nairn IV12 4HW
01667 453119

Corriegour Lodge Hotel
Loch Lochy
Spean Bridge PH34 4EB
01397 712 685

The Creel Restaurant
St Margaret's Hope
South Ronaldsay
Orkney KW17 2SL
01856 831311

The Cross
Ardbroilach Road
Kingussie PH21 1LB
01540 661166

The Dower House
Highfield
Muir of Ord
Ross-shire IV6 7XN
01463 870090

Dunain Park Hotel
Inverness IV3 8JN
01463 230512

Kinloch Lodge
Sleat
Isle of Skye IV43 8QY
01471 833214

Kylesku Hotel
Kylesku
Lochinver
Sutherland IV27 4HW
01971 502231

Leachin House
Tarbert
Isle of Harris HS3 3AH
01859 502157

Loch Bay Seafood Restaurant
Stein
Waternish
Isle of Skye IV55 8GA
01470 592235

The Loft Restaurant
Golf Course Road
Blair Atholl
Perthshire PH18 5TE
01796 481377

North by North West, Pool House
Poolewe
Wester Ross IV22 2LD
01445 781272

Scarista House
Isle of Harris HS3 3HX
01859 550238

The Carnegie Club at Skibo Castle
Dornoch
Sutherland IV25 3RQ
01862 894600

Summer Isles Hotel
Achiltibuie
By Ullapool
Wester Ross IV26 2YG
01854 622282

Other places which, given more space, I would have loved to include

The Albannach, Lochinver, Sutherland (featured in *Scotland on a Plate*, a previous publication by Black & White Publishing) – Tel. 01571 844407

The Applecross Inn, Wester Ross (in the beautiful, remote village of Applecross, they serve delicious food, notable for the local seafood) – Tel. 01520 744262

Boath House, Nairn (also featured in *Scotland on a Plate*) – Tel. 01667 454896

Cleaton House Hotel, Westray, Orkney – Tel. 01857 677508

Coruisk House, Elgol, Isle of Skye – Tel. 01471 866 330

Craigiewood, North Kessock, Inverness-shire (one of the best B&Bs in the Highlands) – Tel. 01463 731628

Crannog Seafood Restaurant, Fort William (good seafood in a wonderful location) – Tel. 01397 705589

Eilean Donan Castle, Dornie, Wester Ross (excellent home baking) – Tel. 01599 555202

The Fishmarket Restaurant, Mallaig (see your food landed from the trawlers) – Tel. 01687 462299

Garramore House, South Morar, Inverness-shire – Tel. 01687 450268

The Glenmoriston Hotel, Inverness – Tel. 01463 223777

The Old Pines, Spean Bridge (excellent restaurant with rooms) – Tel. 01397 712324

The Old Station Restaurant, Spean Bridge (excellent food and delicious cakes and scones) – Tel. 01397 712535

The Plockton Hotel, Wester Ross (very good food in this most hospitable hotel) – Tel. 01599 544274

The Portland Arms, Lybster, Caithness (comfortable, good food and extremely welcoming) – Tel. 01593 721721

The Rendevous Restaurant, Breakish, Isle of Skye (seeking new premises at the time of writing, but Denis Woodtly cooks fish, shellfish and game to perfection!) – Tel. 01471 822001

Seagreen Restaurant, Kyle of Lochalsh (a very good whole food restaurant and bookshop) – Tel. 01599 534388

The Seafood Restaurant, Kyle of Lochalsh (excellent locally caught fish and shellfish, and wonderful home baking) – Tel. 015995 34813

The Three Chimneys, Colbost, Isle of Skye (restaurant with rooms, also featured in *Scotland on a Plate*) – Tel. 01470 511258

Index of recipes